Praise for *The Bargain from the Bazaar*

"In *The Bargain from the Bazaar*, Haroon Ullah has narrated a fascinating portrait of a family set against the backdrop of Pakistan's history and politics. Malala and I both so enjoyed this stunning debut that brings to light so many of the issues that she has devoted her life to seeing exposed and resolved."
                    —Ziauddin Yousafzai, father of Malala Yousafzai,
                            the bestselling author of *I Am Malala*

"As a longtime scholar, diplomat, and writer on South Asia, Haroon Ullah understands the complexities of modern South Asia. In *The Bargain from the Bazaar*, he takes us back to the most romanticized corner of Lahore to show how generational change requires us to shift our focus in understanding modern Pakistan. Neither the lens of Partition nor tensions with India capture the country's profound internal transformations as it grasps for stability. This powerful and gripping account of a family struggle in the middle of chaos fills the void. A must-read for anyone."
                    —Reza Aslan, author of *No god but God* and *Zealot*

"Haroon Ullah has produced a deeply reported and literary work that tells the story of Pakistan's struggles with the promises and perils of modernity and the challenges posed by a rising tide of religious fundamentalism. *The Bargain from the Bazaar* has much to reveal to readers about one of the worlds' most important and volatile states, but it does so in a story that unfolds like a novel."
                    —Peter Bergen, author of *Manhunt: The Ten-Year Search*
                            for Bin Laden from 9/11 to Abbottabad

"*The Bargain from the Bazaar* is an epic telling of family life in contemporary Pakistan from a fresh, sure voice. I read this book in one sitting and thoroughly enjoyed it."
                    —Eboo Patel, author *Acts of Faith* and *Sacred Ground*

"In *The Bargain from the Bazaar*, Haroon Ullah delivers a moving portrait of a family struggling amidst the chaos of living in Pakistan. Ullah's rich storytelling brings the setting to life and helps to illuminate the country's complex history and politics. A wonderful debut from a promising young scholar."
                    —Jared Cohen, founder and director of Google Ideas and author of
                    The New Digital Age: Reshaping the Future of People, Nations, and Business

"A powerful story that fills a real void from one of the best young scholars and frontline diplomats in tumultuous South Asia."
                    —Parag Khanna, author of *The Second World:*
                            Empires and Influence in the New Global Order

the
Bargain
from the Bazaar

the
Bargain
from the Bazaar

A FAMILY'S DAY OF RECKONING
IN LAHORE

Haroon K. Ullah

PUBLICAFFAIRS
New York

PublicAffairs books are available at special discounts for bulk purchases in the United States by corporations, institutions, and other organizations. For more information, please contact the Special Markets Department at the Perseus Books Group, 2300 Chestnut Street, Suite 200, Philadelphia, PA 19103, call (800) 810-4145, ext. 5000, or e-mail special.markets@perseusbooks.com.

Set in 11.75 point Minion Pro by the Perseus Books Group.

Library of Congress Cataloging-in-Publication Data
Ullah, Haroon K.
  The bargain from the bazaar : a family's day of reckoning in Lahore / Haroon K. Ullah. — First edition.
    pages cm
  ISBN 978-1-61039-166-5 (US hardcover) — ISBN 978-1-61039-411-6 (India paperback) — ISBN 978-1-61039-167-2 (ebook) 1. Reza, Awais, 1947- 2. Reza, Awais, 1947—Family. 3. Lahore (Pakistan)—Biography. 4. Middle class families—Pakistan—Lahore—Biography. 5. Merchants—Pakistan—Lahore—Biography. 6. Lahore (Pakistan)—Social conditions. 7. Islam and politics—Pakistan—Lahore. 8. Violence—Pakistan—Lahore. 9. Suicide bombings—Pakistan—Lahore. I. Title.

DS392.2.L3U45 2014
954.91'43—dc23

2013045156

First Edition

10 9 8 7 6 5 4 3 2 1

To Amber, Ami-ji, Abu-ji, and family
and to He who bestows all blessings

ॐ

Author's Note

Since the cataclysmic 9/11 attacks, Pakistan has been the United States' most important regional ally in the long-prosecuted war against violent extremists. Despite the many difficulties in the relationship over the years, the United States has become fully committed to Pakistan. Clearly this commitment was and is a calculated risk. However, prevailing wisdom among many has long concluded that it is Pakistan—*not* Afghanistan—that holds the key to victory over the superpowers of terror.

Pakistan is one of the few nations that is both poverty-ridden and armed with nuclear weapons. Of course, the current political, economic, and social conditions in Pakistan are alarming, and Pakistan remains a nation in transition. Nervous tremors over Pakistan reverberate daily among Washington policy-makers, military shot-callers, and coalition partners. Still, a viable and safe Pakistan is crucial to rooting out and defeating terrorist groups while protecting U.S. security and global interests.

Situated at the center of an active war zone, Pakistan has become a routine international news dateline. Suicide bombers and car bombers have become bread-and-butter fare for the world's news vendors. With all of this public attention, it is not surprising that more and more people are taking an active interest in the Islamic Republic of Pakistan, about which the West knows relatively little. Until recently, it was simply another distant land, hard to find on the map, shabby, with weird music, and full of unpleasant goings-on and lethal behavior. Word is, people simply disappear in Pakistan. A former British intelligence official quipped to a BBC World Service reporter, "I don't know if Pakistan is a country or a missing-persons bureau anymore."

This book is set in the current state of danger. I wanted to reflect the fascinating but unseen Pakistan—the everyday struggles of ordinary middle-class families, which are seldom seen in the news, by telling the true story of one family, the Rezas. *The Bargain from the Bazaar* is the result of eight years of extensive field research conducted throughout the Middle East and South Asia, and my relationship with a Pakistani family. My work included many in-depth interviews with those living inside the turmoil of contemporary Pakistan, from the average family to the man on the street, from the middle-class businessman to the lower-class shopkeeper, from national and regional officials to key political actors. I also conducted several dozen face-to-face interviews with Taliban commanders and their foot soldiers, including those who were once committed to the cause of radicalism but subsequently gave it up to return to their stores and farms.

The individuals depicted here have kindly and courageously given me their valued confidences. I have assured each of them that they will remain anonymous. Therefore, to protect the lives and security of my varied sources and their families and friends, I have changed the names of key family members. The incidents and events in the book are based on detailed, feet-on-the-ground research and hundreds of interviews. I spent over three years in Pakistan between

January 2008 and June 2012, the time frame of the events described in this book. Although I witnessed some of the events firsthand, the dialogue comes from detailed, open-ended discussions with the individuals central to them. Many of these interviews, including the speakers' thoughts, feelings, and introspective comments, are recorded in extensive notes and audio and video recordings. My policy and academic research on the political behavior of individuals and the drivers of extremism in Pakistan dovetailed with my personal work, giving me a clear understanding of what shapes middle-class families and those outside the sphere of wealth and influence.

As an American with South Asian heritage (I grew up in rural Washington state) who visited Pakistan regularly from my earliest years, I have a special feeling for the story of the Pakistani people. I know the language, the culture (or, rather, cultures), what traditions to observe, when to talk, and when to shut up. Over the years, during my many official and unofficial stays in Pakistan, I came to know intimately the urban centers of Lahore, Karachi, and Islamabad, as well as some of the small farm communities that make up the bulk of the nation. I also spent time, often dangerous time, in the insurgent-infested Northwest Frontier Province.

This book is just one family's story from those adventurous years.

ONE

Then which of the favors of your Lord will you deny?

AL-QURAN

A bold sun had clamped down on the city of Lahore that summer day in 1972. In a back alleyway in the Anarkali section, a neighborhood of modest homes and small apartment buildings, the merciless heat had driven almost everyone inside. Few people were around to notice the figure of a man who had materialized out of the blinding sunlight. Slowly he walked along the ancient cobblestones, his steps deliberate and careful. As he emerged from the sun's glare, it was apparent that he was wearing the sand-colored uniform of the Pakistani army with the chevrons of a corporal, a lance naik. The uniform was ragged and filthy, the leggings muddy. The man's toes poked through cracked and split combat boots. He was thin, almost emaciated, and his stringy hair and shaggy beard framed the bombed-out features of a lost soul.

An elderly woman sweeping her doorstep had been watching the man as he shuffled along the alley. As he got nearer, she moved back into the shadows of her doorway, but something made her pause. The man saw her and stopped. He opened his mouth, but no words came out. The old woman set aside her broom and stepped into the alley.

"Can I help you?"

The man strained to speak but couldn't.

The old woman looked him up and down, then eyed his malnourished face. Gradually the shock of recognition began to show in her face. "Wait!" she cried, then rushed across the alley and into a little wood-frame house.

The bedraggled soldier did not move.

In a moment a handsome young woman hurried from the house, the old woman behind her, whispering, pushing her forward. Timidly, with palms pressed together piously, the younger one stared at the man. Finally she turned to the old woman, and they exchanged a few heated words.

Reluctantly venturing closer to the ghostly soldier, the young woman studied him for a very long moment. Abruptly her face became animated, her eyes big and bright as she erupted into tears. "Awais!" she screamed and fell forward, clutching at the man's legs. Her crying quickly became a wailing that echoed down the alley.

"It's him!" someone yelled from an upper floor. "It's Awais Reza!"

∞

THE REZA FAMILY was among the first to become citizens of the new country of Pakistan. They had migrated from Kashmir and Amritsar in north India and settled in the ancient inner core of Lahore following the historic Partition of Pakistan from India in 1947. The Reza family had moved to a land once ruled by a long series of empires, beginning in the eighth century and stretching into the nineteenth. The last of the devout Muslim dynasties, the Mughals, flourished from the mid-1500s to the mid-1800s, when the British took firm control. In 1858, the Crown issued the "Non-Interference Proclamation" throughout its Indian empire, which allowed local regions to organize and regulate commerce without undue imperial influence or interference. This created a favorable environment for Muslims to mobilize around distinct religious identities. However, subsequent ill-advised reforms by the British had powerful, unintended consequences. The Indian Councils Act of 1892 initiated a policy of separate representation on government councils for Hindus and Muslims. The Partition of Bengal in 1905 supported Muslim calls for separate political representation. The Morley-Minto reforms of 1909 further institutionalized religious divisions by forcing Muslims and Hindus to vote in separate electoral blocs.

The resulting political order was separate and unequal. Lines on the map relegated Muslims to the role of a permanent statistical minority in British India. The ascendant Hindu political class took advantage of its majority status and had little incentive to negotiate power-sharing agreements with its Muslim counterparts. This deepening political-religious identity spurred the rise of "confessional" Islamic parties, and over time the political landscape became fully polarized along religious lines.

After World War II, the British lost their will to hold on to India, and indeed their ability to do so. They proposed establishing a loose federation of Indian states with a weak national government of limited powers. But negotiations broke down when Muslim rights and certain traditions could not be guaranteed.

Political squabbling, gridlock, fog, and friction led the British to formally partition India to create West and East Pakistan. The country became a commonwealth in 1947 and the Islamic Republic of Pakistan in 1956.

Like many of Britain's cast-off colonies in South Asia, the independent Pakistan was not created as a true democratic republic. Its system of government was cobbled together from a host of competing traditions, including feudalism, Islamism, and Western-style representational government. Pakistan's political structure from the very beginning was a grab bag of high-minded ideals, local pragmatism, and a need for strength at a vulnerable time.

:∞:

AWAIS REZA WAS BORN in the year of the Partition, 1947, the same year that his family took up residence in Lahore. Lahore was still reeling from the aftermath of violence and bloodshed between Hindus, Muslims, and Sikhs. This ancient Punjabi site had once been the capital of the great Mughal empire. Known as the Paris of the East, Lahore was one of the sparkling jewels of British India; young army officers considered it a choice posting. T. E. Lawrence and many other soldiers journeyed to Lahore for R and R. Indeed, Lawrence was said to have briefly married in Lahore. Over time the city became almost Anglicized in some respects, from architecture to fashion. For more than a hundred years, Lahore was the cultural capital of South Asia, and its polyglot society was well-to-do and cosmopolitan.

However, in 1947, when land was carved out of India during the British withdrawal and the commonwealth was founded, Lahore and other cities became the scenes of ferocious factional fighting. People who had always respected each other's religious freedom, who had lived in harmony for centuries, began turning on each other with sabers and shotguns. Thousands were ruthlessly murdered and thousands more horribly maimed. The upheaval was colossal, like something out of the Bible. The Partition that hacked Pakistan from two sides of India and uprooted more than six million people has been called the greatest landmass transfer in recorded history.

The Reza family walked into the wreckage of Partition, visible everywhere by the time they arrived in Lahore. In those early days, newcomers found accommodation in homes abandoned by owners who had either fled or been killed. The Rezas had cousins already living in Lahore's Anarkali section, so they were able to get settled relatively quickly. However, their new home, a three-room ground-floor apartment, bore disturbing traces of its previous inhabitants. Some of the walls had bloodstains that refused to wash away in spite of repeated scrubbings. It seemed as if the very air were full of terror and heartbreak. As Awais grew up during the 1950s, he heard stories of knife fights, shootings, and murder. Once, near the Anarkali bazaar, Awais's father was an eyewitness when a man casually walked up behind another and shot him in the back of the head. Even in the mid-1960s, old bloodstains and bullet holes were still visible around the city. Partition had spurred the kind of violence that never really washes away. Some nights Awais would lie awake, imagining an unknown boy his own age. Was that his blood on the wall? He often wondered: What was it all about? Why all the hatred? Try as he might, he could never understand killing anyone on the basis of geography, religion, caste, or creed. Yet the aftermath of such killings was all around him.

It was a testing time for a young man, as it was for the young nation. Fortunately, the Rezas were skillful entrepreneurs and had been for several generations in their original homeland in Kashmir and northern India. They had the know-how needed to work the market—any market. The old inner city, including Anarkali, was still a vibrant and lively place in those days, with the bazaar at its hub. It is the largest open market in South Asia, occupying the length and breadth of several inner-city blocks. With seed money from acquaintances who had chosen to remain in India after Partition, Awais's father was able to set up a cloth and rug shop in the bazaar and later expanded it to offer high-end perfume, jewelry, and wristwatches.

Despite the political turmoil, there were opportunities for money-making. In general, the war of the late 1940s and the sporadic fighting in the years that followed did little to damage business throughout Lahore. Indeed, a bit of chaos provided a legitimate opportunity to raise prices.

Working daily beside his father, Daniyal, from the age of twelve, interacting with customers and merchants from all over the region, Awais Reza learned the important lessons and insights of the shop-keeper's trade. "When a man comes to the shop with his wife," his father instructed, "you must immediately decide which of the two has the say-so about money."

"How can you tell?"

"You can't. But if you assume it is the wife, you will be right 95 percent of the time."

"So always play to the wife."

"No. You play to the wife *through* the husband. You act as if he's really the one holding the purse strings, as rare as that would be."

"I don't understand."

"You will if you ever get married." Daniyal Reza reached under the counter and took out a glittering bracelet. "These silver items are more attractive to the female than gold. Why is this so?"

Awais came back quickly: "Because silver is a woman's metal, and gold is a man's metal. You said because silver reflects more light."

His father patted him on the back. "Very good. Now, go un-pack those new throw rugs. And when you put them on the display table—"

"I know. Bright ones on top."

As he grew through his teens and into young manhood, Awais Reza learned from his father all the ins and outs of running a suc-cessful shop as well as the Reza family tradition of fair and honest dealings. "No matter if it be peace or war," the old man would say, "there is always a reliable market for the right goods. The key is to know what the right goods are before the customer knows."

Awais loved the excitement of the busy, noisy bazaar and became friendly with many of the other merchants. From them he learned something of the bazaar's history.

It is uncertain exactly how and when the renowned Anarkali bazaar first came to be a popular trading and retail center. It is likely that distant settlers used the spot as a convenient marketplace, and the venue simply persisted and expanded over the years. There are clear historical references to the bazaar going back at least two centuries. Its narrow, labyrinthine streets are lined with hundreds of tiny shops and stalls with every imaginable offering—books and electrical parts, clothes and cutlery, television sets and motor scooters, and much more. Some shops are tiny "boutiques" selling T-shirts and jeans, while other businesses are larger and fancier, with modern display racks and colorful awnings. Crowds swarm amid the jumble of shops and merchandise. The rickshaws and mini–delivery vans are all adorned with colorful artwork, slogans, and signs and symbols of the trade. The minivans have horns that tap out a musical tune instead of a simple honk. These vans also offer irregular bus transportation for shoppers bound for the bazaar, providing drivers with a few extra rupees.

The marketplace is an assault on the senses. All kinds of food is prepared in front of the customer, from shish kebab to hamburgers, pakoras to samosas. Other stalls are devoted to fruits, vegetables, grains, nuts, dates, figs, olives, spices, sweet treats, and on and on. There are general merchandise shops resembling rundown 7-Elevens. The Coca-Cola Company's famous Spencerian logotype is seen everywhere in both English and Urdu.

Since it is stiflingly hot many months of the year, canvas-topped refreshment booths are everywhere around the bazaar, offering icy lemonade, plum juice, falsa juice, sugarcane juice, and the pride of Lahore, a yogurt-milk drink known as "lassi," which tastes like a tangy milkshake. Husbands who have been dragged along by their wives tend to gravitate to the lassi booths and sit around sipping the "white wine of the East." While the women are off shopping, the men debate everything from cricket scores to the latest government stupidities.

The bazaar opens for business around 9:30 in the morning, and shops often remain open until midnight. Awais Reza liked best the hours after sundown, when the shop was cooler and people were in a better mood to buy. He also liked how the lights and the noise of the Anarkali bazaar drowned out the honking traffic and neon signage from the surrounding metropolis. For Awais, the bazaar was its own little world.

Shop owners would sit outside together in the evening and sip endless cups of tea. While their children played nearby, the men would discuss the business of the day and the affairs of the world. The newspapers were passed around, and the radio gave them the BBC News station. Awais would listen respectfully to his elders but early on developed the habit of forming his own opinions, taking his own counsel. In that sense, he was very much his father's son.

࿐

AT THE TIME OF PARTITION, the newly formed commonwealth of Pakistan consisted of two noncontiguous regions, West and East Pakistan, which were separated by a thousand miles of ancient India. There had always been ethnic and linguistic differences between the nation's two halves. West Pakistan was dominated by Punjabis and Northern Pashtuns, whereas East Pakistan, also known as East Bengal, was the intellectual center of Bengali poetry, arts, and humanities. The politically dominant West had a history of widespread religious and economic discrimination against the Eastern section. In 1956, when the Islamic Republic of Pakistan was formally founded, the leaders of West Pakistan were accused of massive neglect toward the East. Eventually resentment and old feuds boiled over, and agitation and fighting broke out. In a long-building separatist movement led by Sheikh Mujibur Rahman, East Pakistan issued a declaration of independence, which led to the Bangladesh Liberation War. Formal hostilities commenced on March 26, 1971.

Until that time, Awais Reza had been a Pakistani only by the United Nations decree of 1947, not by any special belief or patriotic conviction. His spiritual homeland was still in the lush valleys of Kashmir. But the young country called out to its able men to stand up for the glory of a unified Pakistan. For the first time, Awais was seized with a sense of national pride. And so, heeding his country's call and closing his ears to the advice of his family, Awais enlisted in the army a few months before his twenty-fourth birthday.

The Eastern secessionists had assembled a hardy force of some four hundred thousand troops, and the Western army moved quickly to come up to strength. Awais Reza's company was rushed through boot camp in just four weeks instead of the regulation nine. Those destined for the theater of operations were advanced quickly in rank; in just two months, Awais went from recruit to lance corporal. While home on leave, he met and impulsively married a girl he had just met.

By summer, the new bridegroom was stationed at a garrison inside East Pakistan near the border with India. He might have been green, hardly prepared for warfare, but Awais proved himself an able machine gunner for a mechanized unit. In a single, unforgettable day, he took part in two running gun battles with the well-equipped and dug-in guerrillas. Beyond the battlefields, chaos prevailed across East Pakistan. People murdered and pillaged with a warped and

TWO

I have seen the movement of the sinews of the sky,
And the blood coursing in the veins of the moon.
MUHAMMAD IQBAL

In mid-October 1971, Lance Corporal Reza was among a contingent of soldiers who had surrounded an insurgent camp on the outskirts of Dacca, the largest city in East Pakistan and the rebel capital. What had started out as a straightforward seek-and-destroy mission quickly turned sour when the insurgents launched a surprise counterattack. Awais Reza's squad found itself trapped in triangular fire but managed to stage a bold retreat in armored cars. Even with the rebels swarming everywhere, they nearly made it back to their staging area. But when the ammunition ran out, so did their luck. Many of Awais's comrades were killed in the shoot-out, and the captured survivors were given a stark choice—surrender or die on the spot. Awais and half-a-dozen other men gave up. There was no disgrace in choosing to live.

Lance Corporal Reza and his surviving squad members were held at a repulsive prisoner-of-war camp overflowing with West Pakistan soldiers, where food was scarce, shelter and medical care were nonexistent, and the treatment was brutal. They heard about a preemptive strike made by the West Pakistan air force against a military target, and this gave them a jolt of hope that the rebellion would soon be put down.

That hope was demolished when the Indian army entered the war on the side of Bangladesh on December 3, 1971. This created two fronts, and the Western forces were rapidly outgunned and out-maneuvered—and finally out of time. Late in December, the Allied Forces of Bangladesh and India accepted the formal surrender of the West Pakistan army, resulting in the highest number of POWs since World War II. The apocalyptic civil upheaval had lasted almost nine months. The exact death toll would never be known, but official esti-mates range from two hundred thousand to a ghoulish three million.

The weeks wore on, and conditions at Awais's camp grew worse with every truckload of new prisoners. As 1972 rolled through January, the Western soldiers were still prisoners, and no one knew when they would be released. The war was over, but diplomatic talks were not. Out of sheer desperation, on the verge of starving, Awais and four others used clothing and a camera to bribe a guard to leave a rear gate unlocked.

Late one moonless night, the prisoners escaped by simply walk-ing away. The five soldiers then began a nightmarish, months-long trek across the forbidding, vast enemy territory of India. The escap-ees kept to the wilderness and off the main roads, seeking handouts of food where they could, stealing if they had to. When there was nothing else to eat, they foraged for plants and roots. In the more temperate regions they passed through, they sometimes found a mango or plum tree and gorged themselves on the fruit. In other regions, they fought rain and cold. Always there were long hours of walking, and the constant fear of being caught and sent back to the POW camp. Once they swiped a pickup truck from a remote farm but had to abandon it when the gasoline ran out.

"It will be too much risk going into town for fuel," Awais insisted.

"We don't have a rupee between the five of us. We'd have to steal it."

"Forget such things," Awais said. "We stay safe when no one sees us. That means we must walk."

And so the walking went on and on. The soldiers hid by day, traveled by night, always hungry, with blistered feet, suffering hacking coughs from the cold and damp. They lost track of time and finally of the calendar. When they crossed the border from India into West Pakistan, Awais did not realize it was his twenty-fifth birthday.

∞

SHEZ AKBAR WAS BORN in 1956, just after Pakistan formally became a republic, and grew up in a low-income section of Lahore called Krishan Nagar, which took its name from the ancient Hindu temple of Krishna. Krishan Nagar was originally highly diverse, with Christians, Hindus, and Muslims living and working side by side, but by the late 1950s, it was racked by religious violence rivaling the time of Partition a decade earlier. Shez's father had been a career railroad engineer, but when the rail system was disrupted in the 1960s and the trains couldn't run, he was thrown out of work and had to scrounge around for odd jobs to feed his six children. Shez was the oldest.

Her parents knew that education was the only way for those of their class to climb up in the world. So sacrifices were made and attention focused on Shez. She was a sweet-natured and industrious student with a strong will to succeed, determined to make her parents proud and to help her family survive the harsh conditions of post-Partition Pakistan. Certainly the odds were against her. But she had a few "tricks up her sleeve"—a phrase she had learned from her American pen pal, Lois, in Cincinnati. Through Lois, Shez was picking up not only English-language skills but also a sense of a wider world.

"Let's be realistic," Shez told her mother. "It'll cost too much and take too long for me to become a lawyer or a doctor or anything fancy like that. It's reaching too high."

"Then what do you want to be?"

Shez explained that when she and her girlfriends walked by the big Punjab Medical Center on the way to school, they often saw women in white uniforms scurrying between the buildings. "I want to be one of them, a nurse. I'd like that very much." This was a sensible and attainable goal, typical of Shez's pragmatic personality. So it was more or less settled: Shez would go on to nursing college after high school.

During her early teenaged years, Shez would spend long hours at the library in addition to helping her mother with chores and taking care of her younger brothers and sisters, scolding them when they neglected their homework and praising them when they did well on tests. "If you don't know your lessons," Shez would tell them, "it is an insult to your teacher. That is not a smart thing to do."

When Shez was in her second year of high school, her parents began to be concerned that her studies and career plans might be an obstacle to an even more important ambition. She was spending so much time on academic work that they feared she was jeopardizing her chance for a good marriage. The pretty teenager had already turned down two possible suitors from families in Anarkali. "I have to feel something special for a husband," Shez explained. "Marriage is for life. Please understand; I want to make the right choice."

Shez Akbar was fifteen in March 1971 when the war over Bangladesh broke out. That made her situation more complicated because many eligible young men were off to battlefields in the East, and many would not be coming back. With every passing day, her chances for a good marriage were reduced. Her parents' mood ranged from concern to alarm.

"We have to do something, and we must do it soon," Mr. Akbar said to his wife and daughter.

But Shez was strong-willed, even stubborn, on the subject of a husband. "I won't be like other girls who are forced into an arranged marriage to a man they don't truly love."

"*Love*?" her father scoffed. "In the name of Allah, what does love have to do with it?"

Shez and her mother exchanged looks and burst out laughing.

"Well, I didn't mean it quite that way. Of course love is a factor, among others."

"Didn't you love Mother when you got married?"

"Naturally, but there were other considerations, my child."

"Such as?"

"We don't need to get into all that. You're very clever at changing the subject, aren't you?"

But the subject could not be avoided for long.

One of Shez's schoolmates in Lahore announced that she was getting married and asked Shez to be in the formal procession. "But I have nothing to wear," Shez complained. In fact, she had no need to worry; her mother was an expert seamstress who regularly made school clothes for her three girls. She set about retailoring an old gown of her own for Shez, decorating it with rhinestones and sashes picked up cheaply at the Anarkali bazaar. On the day of the wedding, friends told Shez she was the best-dressed of all the girls.

After the wedding ceremony at the bride's home, the younger boys and girls gathered around the refreshment tables and socialized while the older folks sat nearby, watching to make sure all proprieties were observed. It was then that Shez caught sight of a handsome young man in an army uniform.

She wasn't the only girl who noticed Lance Corporal Reza. Shez and a couple of her girlfriends fell to whispering and giggling, casting occasional surreptitious glances at his handsome features and soldierly deportment. Later, when the party was thinning out and the newly married couple had departed with the groom's family, Shez saw her parents talking to the young soldier. She quickly slipped away from her friends and joined her mother and father. The soldier bowed graciously when they were introduced, repeating her name as though it made him happy just to say it. She was instantly smitten, though too bashful to do more than mutter some pleasantries. "The ceremony went perfectly, don't you think?"

That night she wrote her American pen pal, Lois, and used another phrase the Cincinnati girl had taught her: "love at first sight." That seemed to say it all.

The next morning, Shez's mother called her into the kitchen for a quiet talk. "What did you think of that soldier, Awais Reza?"

Blushing with excitement, Shez could only smile. "Who?"

"Come, now, I saw how you looked at him! Do you think he would make a good husband?"

Shez averted her eyes. "Why? Did he say something?"

"Not to me, but to your father."

"What did he say?"

"I'll let him tell you. He has invited Awais for dinner this evening."

Shez ran outside, where her father was plucking a freshly killed chicken. A whole chicken! Something special was in the works. "Abba, what did the soldier say about me?"

"Nothing, really. Only that he thought your dress was very pretty."

Shez sat down next to him. "That's it?"

"Why? What did you think he said?"

"You are playing games, Abba! Tell me! What did he say?"

Shez's father put the chicken aside and cleaned his hands on a rag. He was silent for a long moment. "Did you like him?"

"Yes; all the girls did."

He put his arm around her and hugged her close. "I think this might be the man we have all been waiting for."

Shez began to weep, and her father kissed her forehead. "We may be poor," he whispered through his own tears, "but Allah has blessed us."

The future was very much on everyone's mind. With Pakistan engulfed in the Eastern war, with men falling in battle at an alarming rate, many weddings were rushed forward with nervous haste, as if this were the last chance for the young to seize their dreams. The wedding of Awais Reza and Shez Akbar took place just a week after their betrothal. As tradition dictated, the ceremony was held at the bride's home, where there was a little garden. It was a lively but low-budget affair. Mr. Akbar had to rent the jewelry that was customary for all brides. Family members and neighbors pitched in to prepare the food, cooking up vats of curries and spicy biryani rice. Shez wore the traditional red gown and Awais was in a white shalwar kameez, the traditional Muslim attire for special occasions. Flowers were sprinkled over the bride and groom as they proceeded to their places before the cleric, who spoke the simple words of sanctification. After the vows of marriage were exchanged, it became a noisy party. It was a joyful occasion, despite the backdrop of a treacherous war, in exuberant defiance of the grim drumbeat of bad news from the East.

Awais's matrimonial leave was cut short by orders from his regiment. The young couple's honeymoon consisted of only two days, and both days were shared with extended family. Shez and Awais barely had time to themselves in the marriage bed.

By December 1971, Awais was a prisoner as Pakistan's war in the East ended ignominiously. While the months wore on and Awais languished in the POW compound near Dacca, Shez gave birth to their first son, Salman, or Sallu, as everyone came to call him.

The Bangladesh war was hard on Shez at home in the Anarkali section of Lahore. Fortunately, living with her in-laws among her and their extended families was a great help, especially with the care of little Sallu. However, she was growing more and more concerned over the abrupt cessation of phone calls and letters from her husband, who had always written several times a week. Her telegrams to army headquarters went unanswered. Sleepless nights and long days began to wear her down. To keep herself sane, Shez had to be out doing something to help people and take her mind off the awful uncertainty of Awais's fate.

"You know I always wanted to be a nurse," she told her mother. "The hospital is offering a special training program. With the war casualties so high, they need a lot of help."

"You are pure goodness. Even as a little girl, Shez, you were always ready to help others. Yes, go help at the hospital. I will watch over the child."

Shez sailed easily through the month of classes and hands-on training and was assigned to one of the wards in the intensive-care unit. She would leave the infant Sallu with her mother, take the bus to the hospital, and work a twelve-hour shift. All of the men in her ward had suffered fearful battle wounds: limbs blown off, skulls bashed in, faces shot away. One young man named Asher had lost both of his legs; he confided to Shez that he had no reason to live because he had trained since childhood to play professional soccer. She heard many more heartbreaking stories. Each day patients would die with hardly a whimper, to be replaced by other broken young soldiers. It was horrible to witness. As she changed bandages and bedpans, spoon-fed the helpless, and kept track of medication charts, Shez was never without thoughts of her missing husband. When she was alone at night on the ward desk, she would shed silent tears, not just for her own loved ones but for all of Pakistan. "Allah, if it should please Thee, deliver us from these troubles," she would whisper.

The end of the war brought more worries as each family waited for their sons and husbands, brothers and fathers to return home. One awful day, Awais's mother received a telegram from the Red Crescent regretfully informing her that he had been killed in a fierce border battle. Shez took the news like a kick in the stomach. But then, after she had made her prayers and promises to God, she announced to the family that it wasn't true, that Awais was alive and would come home. His mother felt exactly the same way. "It is not his time," she declared with finality.

A long period of waiting followed that unnerved the entire clan. Week after week, month after month, there was no news. Shez redoubled her devotions, and Awais's mother continued to insist, "It is not his time." But hope can be sustained for only so long. By the time the war had been over for six months, although no one in the family wanted to speak of it, there was a growing sense that Awais might not come home. Just as Shez was on the verge of accepting that her husband had been gathered back to his fathers and would never return to her arms, her faith was rewarded.

An army colonel in a well-pressed uniform drove into Anarkali and sought out the Rezas. He had news. Awais had not been killed after all! The officer used the word "martyred" and added, "However, he has been taken prisoner and is in a POW camp."

It was all he knew. There was no word of Awais's condition or when he would be released. Though the Rezas were now more hopeful than ever, the agonizing waiting continued. Even the Red Crescent had no information to offer on the fate of POWs in Bangladesh.

One day Shez was sitting at home watching little Sallu when she heard a minor commotion outside and went to the window. In the alley, she saw a ragged, scrawny soldier in a torn and dirty uniform. The old woman from across the way was talking to him.

Suddenly the woman bolted toward Shez's door. "It's him!" she called.

Shez rushed out into the alley.

"See!" the woman cried. "Allah has given you your prayers!"

∞

RELIEVED AND THANKFUL to be home with his family, Awais could see how the nation had changed since Pakistan had lost the war and, with it, half its territory and more than half its population. Bangladesh was a buoyant new country; Pakistan had been humiliated, left friendless in the world to tend its wounds. Gone were the unbridled passion and hope of his countrymen, replaced by provincialism and a warped, desperately distorted interpretation of holy scripture.

Then a further hardship came from an unexpected source. Awais and four of his fellow POWs were arrested because of their escape from the prison camp. They were accused of collaborating with the enemy and disclosing army secrets in exchange for their freedom. The accusations were ridiculous but serious; they constituted treason, which carried the death penalty. Awais and the others, fresh from their grueling escape from Bangladesh, now found themselves jailed in a military prison in their homeland. Awais's father was brokenhearted at the way his son was being treated by the state—so much so that the family believes he simply lost his will to live. He died one afternoon while sitting in the shop at the Anarkali bazaar.

After several hard months behind bars, a trial was finally held. Since there was not a shred of evidence to prove collusion with the enemy and no support for the charge that military secrets had been divulged, all charges were dropped. Awais was released, but he was a changed man, his soul having been damaged by the very government he'd risked his life to uphold. There was a grotesque irony about the business.

Free at last, Awais returned to the shop at the Anarkali bazaar that his father had left him. He kept in touch with his fellow soldiers from the old regiment and even spoke out publicly when President Ali Bhutto rushed forces into Balochistan Province in 1973 to quell an uprising. Awais was deeply saddened by reports of more Pakistanis being killed by their own army.

Pakistanis had lost faith in the whole idea of Pakistan. A degraded nationalism was now afoot in the land, with an increased emphasis on ethnic roots and religious views. Gone was the country's initial burst of esprit de corps. Religious opportunists manipulated the unread masses, and Islam was used by political actors to excuse or attack every problem in society. The federal government issued strict and overbearing new laws and ordinances dictating family relations in marriage, divorce, dowry, and inheritance. The people were heartsick over it all.

"Now we've got real problems," Awais told his fellow shopkeeper Noor.

Noor shrugged it off. "Don't worry; it'll get worse. It always does."

And it most certainly did get worse—much worse. Signs of decay and fading hope were advancing everywhere. The white-and-green crescent-and-star flag of the Islamic Republic of Pakistan, once held in pride and high esteem, now flew in many places at half-mast. At the entrance to the Anarkali bazaar, a flag shredded by disgusted merchants was left on the ground for all to walk on and even spit on. Teenagers were seen urinating on it, the ultimate in disrespect. Ominously, provincial flags were replacing the national ensign all over Lahore and other major cities. A Lahore *Times* editorial headline put it bluntly: "We Are No Longer One Nation."

"There is nothing to look forward to," groused the keeper of the shop across from Awais's store. He wrinkled his nose as if he smelled camel droppings. "This is not the country we signed on for and fought to preserve."

"Our only hope is a return to the old days."

"And how likely is that to happen, Awais?"

"The military will come in again and take charge," another merchant chimed in. "We will have nothing left of the country we used to love. I say *used* to love."

Awais shook his head. "Even our cricket team has lost its supporters. They used to be so damn loud about how great they were. Now the stands are almost empty."

"The press barely mentions the team, hardly reports their games anymore."

"Ah!" Awais erupted. "Who the hell cares about sports when we have to live with all this turmoil?" Awais headed back into his shop. "Pakistan was once a nice dream."

But the Reza family hung on despite the tangled affairs of the nation. Like most small-business owners, Awais coped with the larger world as best he could while staying focused on his family and the shop. The shop was making a profit. Sallu was growing up to be a bright lad. Shez had given up her work at the hospital and was back to mothering and housekeeping full time. In 1978, a second son came along, Daniyal, named after Awais's honored father. Whatever the state of the country, Awais could tell himself that his family was, if not thriving exactly, at least growing, on its feet, and making its way forward. He could be proud of it.

Then came December 24, 1979.

Acting on requests from Afghanistan's Marxist government, the Soviet Union launched military forces into that country to assist in the fight against the mujahideen insurgents who were out to topple the godless communists in Kabul. Ground troops, tanks, and helicopter gunships were deployed around the capital city and outlying regions. At first, in order to disguise the true mission of these units, the government called them "technicians" and "advisers." This thin cover story soon fell apart, and by July 1980, the shooting war was in full swing. In reaction, fighters came from all over, gravitating to Afghanistan to help wage jihad against the Russian infidels. Outgunned by Moscow's seasoned army, the guerrillas reached out for support. It was soon forthcoming from Saudi Arabia; Pakistan; and, covertly, from international allies.

"If the Russians take over in Afghanistan," Awais said one night while watching the news at home, "we will have them on our necks within a year. If the rebels win, we will have the jihadists at our doorstep within six months."

Though his wife was not interested in or educated about political matters, Awais's worries were her worries. "Surely what is happening in Afghanistan will stay on that side of the border. Am I being naive?"

"Yes, my darling, very naive. I'll give you an example. I have always paid a certain fair sum for Afghan woven goods. These are popular and very profitable. But ever since the Russians showed up, the border has become too dangerous for delivery trucks to cross. Only a few get through."

"I have heard about hijackings."

"Every day there are hijackings, Shez. That has made the cost of Afghan rugs shoot through the roof. I can no longer afford to stock them; my customers won't pay those prices. So we lose money. And that's just one item. There are other increases coming that will eat up my profit margin."

The toddler Dani wandered in and climbed onto his mother's lap, babbling delightedly. The older son, Sallu, was busy in the corner playing with the Lego set that had been smuggled in from Bombay. Awais and Shez fell silent and watched the children for a while. Awais sighed. "Maybe they will have a better life," he murmured.

"This is what I pray for."

"As do I."

The disruptive war in Afghanistan raged on. Pakistan aided the resistance while the Russians treated Pakistani sovereignty with utter disdain, crossing the border at will whenever chasing insurgents from Afghanistan. Afghan Muslims looked to their Pashtun brethren in Pakistan's mountainous Northwest Frontier Province for help in the conflict. Among the Pashtuns, there was popular support for a holy war against the Red Army, partly because Soviet socialism was explicitly antireligious and also because the Pashtuns were fiercely independent and had always refused to knuckle under rule from the government in Islamabad, or any authority other than their own tribal leaders. By the middle of the 1980s, insurgents were showing up in most major Pakistani cities, preaching the old line: strict obedience to religious texts against the corrupt. Because of its close proximity to war-wrecked Afghanistan, Pakistan saw a mass influx of desperate refugees, seasoned terrorists, religious outliers, and political fanatics. During this period, Pakistan endured two extended periods of martial law while refugees from the north flowed into Lahore at an alarming rate. Shady, foreign-speaking men with no money or jobs loitered around the Anarkali bazaar. Violent crime, burglaries, and stickups became commonplace. In fact, so frequent was ordinary street crime that the police had to be bribed to investigate or make an arrest.

Through it all, Awais Reza kept his head down, worked hard, and came home every evening. He looked forward to being with his two sons, Salman and Daniyal. In time, a third boy, Kamran, joined the Reza family.

Though he had chosen to ignore the outside world as best he could, that world crept progressively closer to Awais. This was no longer his father's Pakistan. The Anarkali neighborhood of Lahore had slowly but surely changed. Although it was still inhabited by the old families who had settled there at the time of Partition, the easy-money men and the shady characters were beginning to dominate the city. Phony "discount" stores selling overpriced electronics, gray-market goods, and cheap, made-in-China religious icons popped up around the bazaar, hurting legitimate merchants, while drug dealers paid off the police and were given free rein. Anarkali eventually lost its friendly identity, the easy sociability that had once made it such a vibrant community. The cobwebs of neglect were evident all over the inner city, with potholed streets and water pipes bursting weekly. "Going out of business" signs were plentiful. The Reza family and its longtime neighbors found that there was nothing they could do to stop the decay, no way to keep outsiders out. Other forces had taken over and were shouldering aside the old-timers.

THREE

Democracy is the best revenge against dictatorship.

BENAZIR BHUTTO

"Roll me up a banger," Salman told his pal Wazir.

They were at Wazir's house in a quiet back street of Anarkali. Wazir's widowed father was at work in Lahore, and the place was empty. Like many teens hanging out after school in Pakistan's big cities, they were getting high.

"Want to try some meth instead?" Wazir asked. "I just copped a little from the Snake."

"I've never done meth."

"It's a speedy trip, like coke or crack, but it lasts a lot longer. Like all day!"

Salman had stayed away from hard stuff, the opium and heroin smuggled in from Afghanistan. But he enjoyed a hand-rolled cigarette of hashish sprinkled with cocaine. It was the drug of choice for many kids in Lahore because it was relatively cheap and easily available.

"What do you do, smoke it?" Salman asked.

"Yeah. Should I get the pipe?"

"Hell, might as well."

"You'll like it. Does the trick."

Salman Reza had always been the rebellious type. Drug use was not an uncommon rebellion: according to Pakistan's own health minister, fully half of young people between ages thirteen and twenty-two used some type of drug about once a week. This was often blamed on easier access to drugs because of the Afghan war or on the deprivations experienced by the young in a land of few resources and limited opportunities. Young people in Pakistan were under a lot of day-to-day stress and turned to drugs to alleviate the depression and anxiety they felt about their future.

None of this went unnoticed by Salman's parents. Seeing that his son was headed down the wrong path, Awais talked to him now and then about becoming an army officer and making something of himself. The young man did not like the idea. "What did the army ever do for you, Abba?" he asked. "You went through hell for them; then they threw you in jail on a trumped-up charge."

"That was a matter of confused information, a mistake. And it was finally straightened out. I don't hold a grudge, not anymore, and neither should you, Sallu."

"Why should I risk my life for a government that doesn't take care of its own people?"

"That's a perfect reason to join the army. You would be helping the nation. And you'd have a good life as an officer."

Awais kept at it, insisting that the army would be a wise career choice. Eventually, reluctantly, Salman gave in. Using his regimental connections and a well-placed bribe, Awais was able to get his son into the training program at the Cadet College, near Islamabad. Founded on the initiative of General Ayub Khan, at the time commander in chief of the army, it is a boarding high school, the first of its kind in Pakistan, and serves as a feeder program for the service academies. Most of the training is military-oriented, but cadets are offered a wide range of courses and can pursue any field they choose.

Salman spent the next several months in lecture halls and undergoing field exercises, with long hours at the ordnance range. His father believed that he was trying, getting decent grades, at least keeping up. But Salman was just going through the motions and privately told his friends that he hated military school. When Salman was six months into the program, Awais got a call to fetch his son. Salman had been put on report twice for minor infractions, but when he was found in possession of opium, it meant automatic expulsion.

"Damn his eyes!" Awais cursed.

Saddened and angry, he made the long train trip to the Cadet College. When he reached the iron gates, he saw sentries, roving patrols, and other signs of extra security around the campus. The insurgents operating in Pakistan were known to have targeted the institution, an important resource of the military command, because it trained and housed future officers of the "infidel" army. The students were kept close to the grounds, and a dusk-to-dawn curfew was usually in effect. Awais had hoped such a structured environment would help Salman drop his bad habits and buckle down to a fruitful and honorable career. Now their firstborn was being kicked out of school for drugs, and Shez was distraught. "Not my son! Not the little one we received like a blessing."

With embarrassment and shame, Awais presented himself to the commanding officer of the school.

"You understand our position in this matter, Mr. Reza. Your son is not a bad boy, but these are difficult times, and we cannot allow discipline to slip."

"That is understandable. My son has brought disgrace to our family."

"Please don't take it so hard, sir," the officer said. "Your own service to the nation, which I have reviewed, was of such a high caliber that there are few in the younger generation who could hope to come close to such courage and dedication. I was especially impressed with your novel escape from Bangladesh. If it were up to me, I would give Sallu another chance simply because he is the son of such a soldier. But I have my own superiors."

Salman was downcast and quiet as he sat with his father on the train back to Lahore. Over the following days there were arguments, which turned into shouting matches. Awais felt let down, and Salman was angered that his father had not listened to him in the first place. "I *told* you I didn't want to be an army officer. That was your dream, not mine!" For weeks, father and son barely exchanged a word. Sometimes Salman would slam the door on his way out of the house and be gone for long periods.

"Instead of having the honor of a commissioned officer in the family," Awais lamented, "we'll be lucky if he doesn't end up in prison."

Shez disagreed. "Sallu is a good person. He just doesn't know what he wants to do with his life. We must be patient. A young man is entitled to make mistakes."

"Yes, but how many?"

Awais blamed himself as well as his son. In one respect, Salman was right: it had once been Awais's dream to stand among the officer ranks in Pakistan's proud and seasoned army. But the war over Bangladesh had cut short those dreams. He had tried to pass on his own youthful ambitions to his eldest son. Was that so wrong? Perhaps.

Finally Shez took a hand in the situation, quietly suggesting to her son that he offer to help at the shop. His hardworking father could use the assistance, and it would give Salman something useful to do. As he honored his mother and usually bent to her wishes, Salman accepted the arrangement and went to work at the Anarkali bazaar. Awais would be in the shop from morning until afternoon; then Salman would take over and work until closing time.

It was a handy arrangement, even if it did not immediately transform the relationship between father and son—each avoided talking to the other as much as possible. Awais would leave notes: "Show the finer bolts of cloth outside only when the day is overcast." If they had to speak with each other, it was usually strained and awkward. "You left the backdoor open last night, Sallu. I have told you before, double-check the locks as you walk out."

However, after some time had passed, Awais began in small ways to let Salman know that he too had made mistakes.

"I have thought about what you said, Sallu. About how I pushed you into military school. I guess I wanted a life for you that I could not have myself."

Salman responded to the conciliatory tone.

"It wasn't all your fault, Abba. At first I didn't mind it, and I even liked some of the classes, especially history. You know what I hated the most?"

Awais cocked an eye.

"Don't laugh, but I can't stand the sound of gunfire. It's too damn loud."

"That would be a problem for any soldier, wouldn't it? Do you like running the shop?"

"It's more interesting than I thought it would be. Meeting all kinds of new people every day. Yes, Abba, I will make a much better merchant than I would a soldier."

"At least it's not a loud business. Not usually."

They laughed together for the first time in a long time.

And so, by and by, with give-and-take and a little humor, father and son came back to each other. The hurt was allowed to heal.

∞

DURING THIS PERIOD, Pakistan was experiencing a sweeping fundamentalism that by the 1990s had brought about an "Islamization" of Pakistani society. Many of Pakistan's young were turning to Islam as a way out of the political mess and social troubles the country was experiencing without knowing exactly what they were getting into.

Since the Soviet invasion of Afghanistan, a great flood of Pashtun refugees had flowed into Pakistan. These mountain people of eastern Afghanistan came by the millions, and in a very few years, the culture of Pakistan was thrown out of its natural orbit. Without objection from the major Western and Muslim nations, the Pashtuns imported into Pakistan a new and more rigid concept of religion that rapidly took root. Women were suddenly required to wear the full-length burqa, as prescribed by scripture. Billboards had always been a mainstay for advertisers, and there had never been any official regulations controlling what could or could not be depicted. But photographs or illustrations of women were suddenly frowned upon and would often be spray-painted over with graffiti. Men were encouraged and even intimidated to keep their beards unshaven and had to wear turbans or bandanas to cover their heads. Since it was considered by some to be un-Islamic and disrespectful to have the pants leg touch the ground, men were forced to roll up the bottoms of their trousers. Most music was also considered disrespectful, and hard-liners went around physically threatening people who would not turn off their radios and music players. Records, CDs, and fan magazines were burned. Stores that had always played background music were forced to cease such "ungodly" ways. Movies had always been a cheap form of entertainment for the masses, but the extremists insisted that the cinemas be closed. If exhibitors balked at losing their livelihood, their theaters were bombed; going to the movies could be fatal. In a short time, the hard-liners began to exert a stranglehold on certain regions of the country.

Daniyal Reza, who came of age during this era, was typical of the young men who became deeply involved in Islam, encouraged by a group of extreme-minded religious students. It wasn't long before he joined a madrassa in Lahore headed by a fiery, proselytizing mullah. A major step in Daniyal's radicalization came when he dropped out of school to put all of his energy into following the pure Islamic way of life.

His parents were appalled.

Going to school with girls was against religious principles, Daniyal maintained. "Understand, Abba. There is no need for an English education when all that any of us will ever require is in religious texts."

"I do not disagree that a pious life is desirable, but extreme religious views are contrary to Allah's wishes," Awais quietly contradicted his son.

"What is 'extreme' about obeying God?"

"God can be obeyed in many ways, Dani. Sometimes people go too far, beyond what Allah asks of us."

Salman took his father's side and tried to talk Daniyal out of his zealotry, but the young man could not be persuaded. Daniyal was devoted to the teachings of the mullahs. He would disappear for a

FOUR

I can't let my mother's death have been in vain.
Democracy is the best revenge, and we will have it.

BILAWAL BHUTTO ZARDARI

By 2008, the youngest of the Reza sons, Kamran, was a third-year law student in a scholarship program that allowed him to just squeak by. Unlike his brother Daniyal, he had put his faith in law and order as a means for social change. In Professor Jalees's criminal statutes class, he rose one day and spoke with passion: "Pakistan must change radically. Otherwise we won't survive."

"Hear! Hear!"

"Speak of it!"

"But violence won't get the job done. In fact, it's totally counter-productive. The extremists are turning off more people than they attract."

"That's a fact!"

"They make a big show of their 'learning' within the pages of al-Quran," Kamran went on. "Their learning! As they say in English, they are 'Bible–thumpers.' Few of them have even read al-Quran in its various forms, let alone in its more 'objective' translations." He turned his palms up with lawyerly directness. "Let's face it; the militants aren't just terrorists. They're also an organized crime syndicate. Everybody knows about the American gangsters in Chicago years ago, Al Capone and those people. They used fear and savagery as a way to put millions in their coffers—and our modern-day terrorists do the same thing! We all know they get big funding from regimes like Iran, like Saudi Arabia, certainly from Hamas, even some parts of our own government. In a way, the top-level men in the terror groups are as bad as the Christian evangelists in the States who preach love and charity while living like kings in huge mansions, chauffeured around in luxury cars. Meanwhile, the poverty rate in the United States is shockingly high for the world's reigning superpower. The point is, the higher-ups in the Taliban and their ilk, the top leaders, are not in the killing racket for purely religious and political purposes. They're also in it for the money, the perks."

"Bravo, Mr. Reza," Professor Jalees said as Kamran resumed his seat. "I couldn't have said it better myself, with one exception. The Taliban and the wannabes are acting not only on a quasi-profit motive but one that is made feasible mostly by the use of some child labor. Can anyone name the statute under the Pakistani criminal code that applies here? No? Well, neither can I. But it's in there somewhere."

As usual, Jalees's humor was met with laughs.

"I have seen some rather shocking statistics developed by our political science wizards down on the third floor. It appears that nearly two-thirds of all Taliban, al-Qaeda, and Haqqani foot soldiers are in fact *teenagers*. Teenagers." The professor paused longer than necessary, then raised his Groucho Marx eyebrows with trademark sarcasm. "Hmm . . . A bunch of high school boys . . . uh-huh . . . hopped up on hashish. So these are your suicide bombers, your assassination squads. Comments?"

Kamran and his friend Zain, a political science major, hung out together and enjoyed debating all kinds of things, but mostly politics and religion. They disagreed on some matters but agreed on one thing: the country was at the edge of a precipice. Written off countless times as a failed state, Pakistan had so far defied the pessimists, and the odds, as it continued to survive—though just barely. Family bonds and kinship, the glue holding the whole social fabric together, were losing their grip in a broken economy under the onslaught of violent gangs and corrupt officials. People everywhere were becoming divided by religious ideas.

"People are getting crazy with this strict religious stuff," Kamran said to Zain as they sat together in the dormitory.

"My neighbor Hussein—you remember Hussein, the rickshaw driver? He won't let a woman hitch a ride unless she's with a male relative. Not because he thinks it's wrong but because he was shot at when he had a lone woman for a fare," Zain said.

Kamran shook his head in dismay. "Stupidity."

"But the government is so fucking weak they can't do much to stop the violence."

"Actually, that's not even our biggest problem. We're more threatened by inflation, fraud, street crime, and corruption than we are by the insurgents. The way it is now, Z, the average man has to bribe and smuggle in order to survive on a daily basis. If we could only concentrate on fixing the economy. Of course, that's the last thing the radicals want."

"And the politicians as well. If things get better, their under-the-table payments will be reduced. Not eliminated, mind, just reduced."

After years of living under several military dictatorships, most people had originally applauded Pakistan's drift toward a fully democratic society. It sounded good, but the widespread feeling since the 1990s had been rampant disappointment.

Inflation was out of control, with the cost of food staples soaring out of reach even for middle-class families like the Rezas. Refugees in the influx from Central Asia and China were smuggling in manufactured goods of all types, which quickly began to destabilize the prices of domestic producers. Chinese knock-off brands of television sets and mobile phones severely damaged the market for Pakistan's legitimate manufacturers and importers. Businesses also suffered from a lack of an efficient regulatory infrastructure. The lines of people waiting at administrative offices for every type of license or permit that was required would extend out into the street like ticket holders at a soccer match. It could take hours or even days to get a simple permit to hire an extra employee or expand inventory. Historically, land disputes had always been a major issue in Pakistan, but these frequently ground to a judicial halt—not because of the backlog but simply because the government ran out of printed forms. Civil court cases that should have been resolved in a few days dragged on from month to month and even year to year. On the other hand, if the parties could afford an envelope for the judge and a few other functionaries, the case might proceed with uncommon speed.

Refugees wandered the streets of the big cities, especially around restaurants, seeking handouts, food, and work; sometimes these encounters turned violent. The number of burglaries and armed robberies rose to an all-time high. Anyone holding valuables such as jewelry or cash (most banks were no longer seen as secure) was forced to hide or lock up everything at home. Even longtime servants were no longer trusted. Murder for hire became a light industry, and kidnapping for ransom became a profitable trade. Jails and prisons were permanently filled to capacity, resulting in deadly riots. Officials and the police liked the action, with more and more people forced to pay them for "favors." The incumbent administration, no matter what faction was in power, was simply not equipped to deal with the burgeoning problems threatening the nation. With no widespread support and much to do, each new government became overheated and ultimately overwhelmed.

In contrast, the extremists were seasoned and well-equipped, with grassroots links and supply-chain avenues that had not been closed when the Soviets had abandoned Afghanistan. They were led by the same "freedom fighters" that the United States had initially supported and supplied to resist the Russians. After Moscow withdrew its forces from Afghanistan in 1989, the guerrillas were suddenly enemies of the West. Pakistan became an auxiliary player, to a great extent a reluctant one, in the Afghan war that its U.S. partner was waging against former allies. The unpopular and complicated entanglement with the heavily armed U.S. forces did nothing to enhance the image of a democratic and independent Pakistan. Many saw their leaders, whether civil or military, as mere stooges of Washington. And it didn't help matters when it was widely reported that the majority of Pakistan's parliament consisted of very wealthy men (as if that were a shock to anyone paying attention). The stink of bribery and kickbacks wafted through the halls of official Pakistan like manure behind a carriage horse.

There was a widespread understanding among the people, even the vast number of uneducated, that the violent extremists plaguing Pakistan were crazed fanatics—some homegrown, some imported— who were hell-bent on establishing one form or another of religious law, a version of a theocratic society, regardless of what the majority of the nation wanted. The periodic suicide bombings at shops and government offices were an effort to intimidate ordinary citizens.

People were forced to take sides; being neutral was no longer a viable option. One could not tell friend from foe, neighbor from enemy. Pakistani society had fragmented. And every time there was a bombing, the central government looked more and more inept.

∞

KAMRAN REZA HAD a good idea of what he was going to do with his life after obtaining his degree. He would set about wrangling a post in the national government. But he wouldn't take just any job; he wanted a position that would feed into a fast-track career. Along with most of his classmates, Kamran had a wholehearted goal of bringing honesty and justice into vogue to rid Pakistan of the corrupt officials and military leaders who had grown fat at the expense of the masses. These men were opportunists in the worst sense, looked upon by many as little better than common hoodlums. Like all Pakistanis, Kamran had daily experience with street-level corruption. Growing up around the Anarkali bazaar, he had seen his father and other business owners pay steep bribes to greedy politicians, brutal police officers, and grabby wholesalers just so they could keep their shops open. Kamran knew the top-to-bottom housecleaning that Pakistan needed would be drastic, painful, and dangerous to implement. He realized that true and lasting reform could be accomplished only by those working from within and acting *for* an elected government. He and his peers would have to become part of the nation's elite, as distasteful as that might be, in order to bring about substantive change. It would take time, but they were young, and more importantly, they had the intense desire, the pressing need, to help forge a better Pakistan.

"Of course," Kamran told Zain, "it will take more than idealism to put this country on its feet as a functioning democratic society. A hell of a lot more."

"That is certainly true. Idealism has been tried, and it hasn't worked." Zain shook his head sadly. "And here we are, all thumbs-in-vest over our nuclear arsenal. What a joke that is! As bad as North Korea with its starving masses."

"We can never use the nuclear option," Kamran said. "It would trigger a doomsday scenario that Pakistan could not survive."

"Nuclear weapons are good for nothing but saber-rattling."

And then there was always the United States to worry about. Kamran and friends wondered how long Washington would continue to look the other way, knowing damn well that elements of Pakistan's military and intelligence agencies were channeling aid to Taliban, al-Qaeda, and Haqqani forces. There was a strong sense that the Americans might get fed up and turn on them. What exactly they would do was anyone's guess, but it would come suddenly, unexpectedly—one could count on that.

∞

PAKISTAN WAS IN TROUBLE and had much to deal with and much to worry about. Yet, even in the midst of all the turmoil and fear, a kind of "normal" life went on. Kamran Reza was no different than college boys the world over: he had a sweetheart.

Rania Omar was from a well-to-do family that had also lived in Lahore for several generations. Her father was a high-ranking regional bureaucrat, and her mother owned a fashionable boutique in an exclusive area downtown. As the family's only female child, Rania was pampered, if not spoiled, given advantages that the great majority of Pakistanis could only dream about—a fine home, nutritious meals, servants and chauffeur-driven cars, clothes from Paris and New York.

Rania was in a couple of Kamran's legal classes, and he saw her every day. Her background and higher social status made her somewhat intimidating, so at first he simply avoided her. Even though he was impressed by her striking looks, Kamran was sure the two of them would have little in common. He was a struggling scholarship student who had to take the bus and whose used textbooks were dog-eared. Rania arrived at school in the safety of a Mercedes sedan every morning and had the latest laptop and smart phone. To Kamran, she was part of a world light years from his daily life.

However, as classes and lectures progressed during the year and Rania began to participate in discussions and debates, which could become strident arguments, Kamran began to see a side of her he had not anticipated. She was an opinionated young woman. She had genuine empathy for the underdog and took a special interest in the rights of the poor and the disadvantaged, the underclasses. "If we short-change those stuck at the bottom of society," Rania argued one day in class, "we will have failed in our responsibility to the best traditions of the legal profession."

It eventually became clear to all that Rania Omar might have been born to great privilege, but she wasn't going to lean on that. Like her classmates, she was ready to roll up her sleeves and help Pakistan come to terms with the modern world.

"I think she's actually got a heart under that expensive cashmere sweater," Kamran confided to Zain.

"It'll never work."

"What? I didn't say anything."

"Never mind."

One day in the student lounge, Kamran complimented Rania on the way she had argued a fine point of immigration law in class that morning. It started a conversation in which Kamran learned that Rania's parents had originally wanted her to go to Oxford or Cambridge for a classic English education.

"But why should I? Pakistan is my country. My family's country. We have good schools right here."

Kamran was especially interested when Rania told him she had declined an arranged marriage with a distant cousin. "My parents weren't very pleased, but they've almost come to accept my independence. Almost." Her smile hinted at a lot more than she was saying.

After that, Kamran and Rania had tea together now and then at the cafeteria at the Student Center and told each other more about their lives. Sometimes they walked around campus together, discussing everything from corporate law to pop music. They didn't exactly fall in love but sort of slipped into it.

Late in the semester, Kamran and Rania found themselves sitting together in the cafeteria. He could tell that she was preoccupied. They had just sat through a long lecture on the judicial aspects of the government's new counterterrorism policies. Ordinarily, Rania would be bubbling with thoughts and opinions, but she remained quiet as she sipped a Coca-Cola.

"All right, pretty girl. What's on your mind?"

"Nothing. Why?"

"Come on, did I say or do something dumb?"

"No, it's not you. . . . If you must know, it's my mother."

"Not the marriage thing again."

Rania laughed sourly. "Yes, the marriage thing again. She's got another fellow picked out for me. This time it's the son of her best friend. He's a nice guy but not my type. Mother thinks he is a perfect match."

"And your father?"

"Him? I told you, he washed his hands of the matchmaking business last year. He's kind of on my side most of the time, but it causes arguments with Mother."

"Let's see; that's what, the third guy she's set her sights on?"

"The fourth if you count my cousin's fifteen-year-old son." Rania eyed him across the table. "Last night I had a talk with her."

"And? . . ."

"I told her I wanted to marry you."

"Really?" Kamran smiled broadly. "Let me guess. She threw you out of the house and disowned you."

Rania giggled. "No, but she did say I was making a mistake."

"Maybe you are."

Rania sagged. "Don't you want to marry me?"

"Of course; I've told you that many times. But your mother might be right. You know my background. Where I come from. I'm here on a scholarship, and my parents can barely afford that."

"I don't care," she said. "Happiness is what matters. Not how much money we have."

"But getting married is a major step. Besides, Rania, it will take time. I have to finish my schooling and get a job. We will have to live on what I make, not what your family has."

"So? We'll be no different than the others at school. Everyone has to work for what they want in life. And don't forget, I'll be bringing in a paycheck too."

Kamran watched her and took it all in. "What do you suggest we do?"

"My mother lives in a fantasy world of weddings and families uniting and all that old-fashioned stuff. So far I've put up with it. But now I think we should go ahead and tell our parents that we are committed."

"Committed? You mean like to an insane asylum?"

Rania grinned mischievously. "Who needs an asylum? I can always count on you for a little insanity."

With their relationship going so well, Kamran was floating on air most of the time. But he was in for a rude surprise.

One afternoon he was leaving a lecture hall and walking back to his dorm to meet Zain, his head full of questions for an upcoming test that afternoon. Out of the campus crowd, a heavyset and bearded young man came forward and blocked his path.

"Listen, *you*! If you persist in insulting the ways of Muhammad, you will be punished." With that, the man rammed his hefty shoulder into Kamran's chest, knocking him to the ground.

Kamran looked up at the assailant. "You crazy fool!"

"You must learn that unmarried men and women do not mix openly. It is forbidden!" The young bully marched off, muttering, "You have been warned."

FIVE

No nation can rise to the height of glory
unless your women are side by side with you.

MUHAMMAD ALI JINNAH

In the old section of Anarkali where Awais and Shez Reza lived, the surrounding streets were aged and worn, ancient and slovenly facades of redstone jammed side by side with dilapidated structures of wood, brick, and plaster. Everything showed the effects of years of havoc, air pollution, and commotion, and it seemed as if a song of sadness were always playing somewhere. At night, the area became a flashing-neon free-for-all. Noise levels were highest at midday but not much lower most other times. Smells were exotic and obnoxious, a mixture of incense and perspiration, exhaust fumes, and fried food. A film of microdust settled everywhere and anywhere. Three- and four-story apartment complexes hung precariously over minishops lining narrow streets and undrained lanes.

The pavement, the curbs, the doorsteps were all worn down to deformity. Every street was crowded and haphazard, the space overhead dominated by garish advertising signs hung out like flags. Swarms of dented small cars, vans, and two-stroke motorbikes coughed along the streets. To Western eyes, the scene had the look and feel of a carefully contrived Fellini movie set depicting some postdoomsday future in which the whole world had gone to seed and nobody cared anymore. Hopelessness ruled alongside toil and want.

Awais and Shez Reza's home was situated in an almost quaint back alley that was swept daily by old women and young children, traditional partners in labor. Colorful Mughal-style paintwork on doorway arches and wooden window shutters gave the street a sagging dignity. Years earlier, Awais had borrowed from an uncle to purchase the one-story, four-room house. It was one of the better homes along the alley, well built and just a twenty-minute walk to the Anarkali bazaar. The rooms were always kept neat and tidy; the divans and other furniture were old but originally of high quality, symbols of the solid middle class to which the Reza family had once belonged. They had been slipping in status over the past decade. "Why complain when we are just one family among many?" Awais always said, echoing his late father.

On a night in September, Awais and his wife were in the living room watching a dubbed British program on their big-screen Sony knock-off television set. Two electric fans at each end of the room wafted the sandalwood incense that Shez liked to burn in the evening.

"And what shall we do for your birthday?" Shez asked.

"Please, nothing special."

She shook her head. "Nothing special? My dear slowpoke husband, this will be your sixty-first birthday. That's a very important milestone."

"Wouldn't *sixty* be the milestone?"

Shez sat up and looked at him in the light from the TV screen. Somehow she still retained her slenderness and the classic good looks of her youth. "But it is not *just* your birthday. You know very well what I mean."

"You bring it up every year, so how could I forget?"

She sparkled with pride. "Another anniversary of your return from the long walk. The thousand-mile walk back to my arms. Let's do something special this year."

"If you insist," Awais said. "At least I won't look quite as bad as I did that day I came home." He grinned. "Remember how awful I smelled?"

Shez burst out in laughter. "You did stink, I must say. But I was so happy to see—" She frowned at the TV. "Oh, *no*, what's this?"

A special bulletin interrupted the British program. There had been a massive bombing at the Sufi shrine. Awais turned up the sound as the somber anchorman broke the news: "The Sufi shrine was rocked by two explosions this Thursday evening—the traditional night when the poor gather for devotion and free food. These back-to-back suicide bombings have killed at least forty, with the injured estimated at over seventy-five. These numbers will certainly rise. Here's what has been learned up to this minute. . . .

"A pair of terrorists wearing vests packed with explosives blew themselves up at different locations within the shrine. The first explosion occurred in the basement just after 9:00 P.M., while the second blast came minutes later in the crowded courtyard. The authorities believe the bombers were very young men, probably teenagers. As of now, there have been no claims of responsibility."

For the weary people of Pakistan such as Awais and Shez Reza, it no longer mattered who took responsibility for the killings. Sudden death and destruction had become as common as the bribes one paid to survive. The people were used to disaster. But the attack on the iconic shrine was a new type, a more blasphemous act of violence. Literally nothing was sacred anymore.

The television images cut to footage showing bodies on the ground and emergency vehicles moving in and out of the area.

As Awais watched the dreadful news unfold, Shez went into the kitchen to make her special milk tea, doodh patti, her remedy for tension and stress. The frightening regularity of violence in Pakistan in recent years had meant that they consumed a great deal of doodh patti.

Awais reached for his Nokia mobile telephone, checked the charge, and punched in a number. "I want the boys to come back home. All three of them. Just to be on the safe side. No telling what the situation will be now." He grimaced as he heard the whining tone on his cell—the tower signal was gone. Five minutes later, the electricity went off, killing lights, TV, and fans. There was complete darkness.

"I'll do the candles this time," Shez called out from the kitchen.

"No matter what happens," Awais complained, "these asses at the power station never forget to shut down at eleven. God take them!" He shrugged to excuse his profanity. "Surely Allah will watch over the boys."

Shez came in with lit candles in a porcelain dish, which she placed on the table. In the dancing light, she looked from the blank TV screen to her husband. From beyond their walls, they could hear a distant hum that sounded like the low moaning of a million huddled souls.

∞

SOMETIME AFTER MIDNIGHT, Kamran got through to his father on a landline from the Student Center. "Good, the cell towers are back up. Have you heard from Sallu or Dani?"

"Nothing," Awais said. "And that worries me. Sallu was at the shop. Dani is probably at his hostel. The cell signals aren't working very well, and I'm running out of battery power."

"I'll go over to the bazaar and see what's happening. Then I'll find Dani."

"Yes, and right away, Kami. Bring both of your brothers here to the house tonight. Take a taxi on me."

"All right, I'll leave now. Zain has his scooter."

"Imagine it! The shrine, of all places to bomb. Killing the poor and the innocent. It's monstrous, monstrous!"

"Yes, it's awful, Abba. I'll see you later."

At that point, Awais's mobile powered out. He tossed it aside, resigned and disgusted. "Sallu was at the shop all day waiting for that perfume shipment. He knows I've already paid the middleman his *hafta*. Why hasn't he called?"

Shez was lighting more candles. "But the phones aren't working right. Let us think positively. I'm sure Kami will find the other boys. They're both a good distance from the explosions."

Awais turned on a little battery-powered radio, and the couple sat listening to the latest news.

ﻼ

BEFORE HEADING TO the Anarkali bazaar to find Salman, Zain drove Kamran on his scooter over to the shrine for a look.

"It's almost a duty to witness something like this," Kamran said. He knew Zain was sometimes sympathetic to the extremists, but he was also pragmatic and highly intelligent and had a good heart. They had had many heated discussions over Pakistan's "destiny," over politics, over violence versus nonviolence as an instrument of change. The deeply felt exchanges had actually strengthened their friendship. Theirs was a bond forged in intellectual kinship and mutual respect.

There was a huge crowd at the site of the bombing, barely held in check by police lines. As usual, it was a melee. Medical units, official cars, and half-a-dozen news vans cluttered the scene. One section of the outer brick wall had caved in, giving the old house of prayer an outrageously vandalized aspect. It was as shocking as if someone had taken a wrecking ball to one of the great cathedrals of Paris or London.

Kamran and Zain watched as ambulances were loaded with broken and bleeding victims, then rushed away with sirens warbling. For centuries, the shrine had been a major pulse point in the life of Lahore, no matter how modern and sophisticated the sprawling city had become. It was the last place anyone would have expected to die.

The two college students were aghast at what they saw, the scale of death and destruction. "You have to ask even though it sounds naive," Kamran said. "Why?"

"Religious differences, I'd say. The hard-liners take the position that worshippers at a Sufi shrine are practicing a distorted conception of Islam. An insult to Allah." When Kamran rolled his eyes, Zain added, "It is a sin, my friend. And sins are punished."

"Not always. And not this way. Killing innocent people."

"You have to understand, Kam, this is a Barelvi shrine. The Taliban believe that is not true Islam. They maintain that the Sufis and the shrine worshippers are violating the holiest of laws." He threw his hands up. "At least that's the party line as I read it."

They fell silent while a bleeding little girl lying on a gurney was trundled past them and lifted into an ambulance. As it sped off, siren screaming, Kamran shook his head in deep disgust. "Let's go. I've seen enough."

∞

SOMETIME AFTER 3:00 that morning, as Awais and Shez were dozing fitfully on the sofa, the electricity sputtered back to life. The table lamps, the fans, and the TV came on all at once. Awais was instantly awake.

The nightly ritual began: plug in the cell phone, set it for rapid charging, and hope to Allah the power held. Sometimes so many people were doing the same thing all over the city that they over-loaded the system, and the electricity went off again. The trick was to do it quickly, as soon as power was restored, going for a fast charge. If that worked, one switched over to the extended-charge mode and crossed one's fingers.

Shez sat up on the sofa, yawning, rubbing her eyes. "What are they saying on the TV?"

The set was still tuned to the Geo News channel, which was running Al Jazeera video of the bombing. Awais used the remote to turn up the volume as the picture cut to a high-ranking official in Islamabad who was detailing the steps being taken to track down those behind the attack.

"They know who is responsible," Awais said heatedly. "But they're afraid to go after them. Because they know the trail will lead right back to their own doorstep."

Voices filtered through from outside. Shez sprang to the window. "They're here!"

In a blink, Awais went from righteous anger to grateful piety, pressing his palms together, mouthing a prayer.

Hugs and kisses followed as the three sons filed through the door. Even Daniyal, usually so standoffish, embraced his parents with affection.

"I told you I'd find them," Kamran said.

"And thanks be to Allah everyone is safe," Shez said.

"We were not in danger, Ammi," Salman told her.

"Sallu, I must ask. What about the perfume shipment?"

"Everything's okay, Abba. I spoke with the broker. Because of

the bombing, they were not delivering tonight. Tomorrow maybe."
This was good news. Sometimes shipments disappeared in transit,
even after a nonrefundable bribe had been paid. "If not tomorrow,
the next day."

"Very well. Let us hope it is so."

The night was still warm, but the revived electric fans offered
some relief. Salman, Daniyal, and Kamran settled in the living room
with their father. Shez hurried into the kitchen to heat up a pot of
lamb stew. "I hope everyone is hungry." She was in a good mood. It
had been a long while since the whole family had gathered together
for a meal.

Awais threw a hand at the news on TV. "This is madness, utter
madness. The country will dry up and blow away if we allow things
like this to continue. They're destroying all we have worked for over
the last sixty years."

"The question is," Salman said, "who can stop them?"

"No one," Daniyal replied. "It will go on until there is a true
Islamic government in power. Then there will be no reason for the
attacks."

Kamran objected, "Oh, come on, Daniyal. There's never a good
reason for killing innocent people."

"Obviously those behind the bombing had a reason."

Awais leaned forward pointedly. "And, may I ask, what reason
would that be?"

"That's not hard to figure, Abba. The Sufi shrine has long been a
blasphemy upon Islam. It was bound to be a target sooner or later."

"But what does it accomplish?" Salman asked.

"Fear and terror," Kamran said. "That's their whole purpose."

Daniyal shook his head. "Not fear and terror—purification.
Allah will accept no less."

"Who says this?" Awais asked.

Daniyal shrugged. "Our leaders."

"Sometimes even our leaders do not understand the ramifications of such actions."

"Oh, they understand, all right. The leaders of the faith have spent years studying religious scripture. They know better than all of us that the will of Allah cannot be denied. It is inevitable."

"Let us not argue these matters," Awais said. "Truly speaking, Allah has plans for everyone. Our destinies have been set."

"Of course this is true, Abba," Daniyal said. "And in religious texts it is written that we must live under Islamic law and no other. The guidance is very clear on this."

"But what kind of Islamic law?" Kamran asked. "The Islamic law of truth and justice? Or the Islamic law of intolerance and cruelty?"

Daniyal looked away, lost in his thoughts. "Perhaps it will require some of both to bring Pakistan to its senses. After that, I assure you, all will be peaceful and serene. True harmony."

Kamran was getting annoyed. "Harmony? Every day we hear about women having acid thrown in their face. Fingers and noses cut off. Women being strangled, raped. I myself have even been bullied by these so-called fundamentalists. And who does these things? It's always some character who claims there was a violation of strict Islamic law. Is that what we want for modern Pakistan—mutilation, murder?" He nodded at the TV. "Dozens of innocent people killed just to make some religious point? That's medieval stuff."

Daniyal sneered at the TV. "You call them 'innocent.' In fact, they are enemies of the sacred light. That school of yours has kept you from a true understanding of Allah's will."

"You could use some schooling yourself," Kamran snapped.

"So I can be stupid like you?"

"Boys, *boys!*" Awais cut in.

Shez called out from the kitchen, "Stop arguing, children, and set the table."

໒໐໑

THE MORNING AFTER the bombing, the bazaar in Anarkali was slow to come to life. Within the tiny streets and cramped shops, merchants were setting up their display goods, and the deliverymen were unloading stock from minivans. Enticing smells gradually filled the air as those catering to the breakfast crowd stirred pots of lentils and fired up the coal grills for the popular meat pies and cinnamon thins. Here and there, people gathered in small groups, discussing the dreadful events of the night before. The hustle and bustle were comforting. Everyone hoped that life around the bazaar would go on as usual. It always did.

Awais Reza had turned on the lights in his shop an hour later than normal. His father had always preached that long hours were the successful shopkeeper's best friend. That wise and kind soul would have been sickened by what had happened at the shrine. Awais went into the tiny back room and set the teapot on the hot plate. He followed the same morning routine his father had practiced for decades. Awais remembered how they would sit with their tea and his father would tell him about the early years in Lahore. His father had especially liked to talk about the mysterious history of the bazaar.

The origins of the marketplace were shrouded in half-truths, myth, legend, and outright poppycock. No one knew exactly, or even approximately, how it had come into being. During the Mughal empire, in the time of Shakespeare and Elizabeth I, the beautiful slave girl Anarkali had been caught with the emperor's son in an illicit romance. For her sins, she was supposedly buried alive, a tabloid detail

that found its way into all versions of the story. The white mauso-
leum in Lahore was said to be her tomb, though the building now
housed the regional records office. Like his father, Awais had always
taken great pride in the Reza family's association with the old marketplace, the most famous bazaar in all of South Asia.

Also like his father, Awais now found that he was frequently
looking to the past, which seemed strangely inviting, despite all the
tears of yesterday.

A bell on the door chimed, and Awais went to meet his first customer of the morning with the set greeting his father had often used:
"Allah has directed you to the right shop, my honored friend."

∞

SHEZ REZA HAD had little sleep that night and awoke feeling groggy.
Having the three boys together for a meal was always a reason for
joy, but the killings at the shrine had made a somber occasion of it.

As she dressed, Shez peered out through the window blinds.
Nothing looked right. There were very few people out on the streets,
which ought to be crowded at this hour. It looked as if everyone were
staying inside. The attack on the shrine had brought widespread
fear. Lahore had been spared much of the militant violence of recent
years, but this bombing was a signal that the distinguished old city
was catching up to the rest of the country's misery.

Shez moved slowly into the kitchen, her arthritic knees creak-
ing. The pain she never complained about was worse this morning;
in fact, everything seemed worse this morning. She put on a fresh
pot of chai and sat at the kitchen table. Had the whole world gone
mad? Would there never be an end to the violence, the shootings, the
bombings, the killings of good and worthy people? Awais had called
it "monstrous," and that was the right word. Only monsters would be
so cruel and heartless.

There was a knock at the back door, and she dried her eyes. It was Gogi, the bucktoothed milkman.

"Good morning to you, Mrs. Reza."

"Hello, Gogi," Shez said listlessly, taking the large milk pot from the cupboard and putting it on the table.

As Gogi hauled his aluminum delivery keg into the kitchen, he was not in his usual boisterous mood. "Have you noticed?" he asked, looking out through the window over the sink. "Where is everyone?"

"They're scared, Gogi. This is a bad time for Lahore."

"A bad time everywhere, you ask me." He started filling the pot from his keg. "On the news, they say a Taliban fringe group is claiming responsibility for the bombing."

Shez shook her head sadly. "I don't care who takes responsibility. I hate them all the same."

"That's what my boss said this morning. Nobody cares who is behind these bombings. Whoever they are, they are the worst people in the world." He finished filling the milk pot and sat down at the table. He was a simple soul. "I don't know what to think anymore. Between the terrorists, the Americans, and our stupid leaders, we're caught in the middle. I heard there was another attack yesterday by one of those flying bombs the Americans use."

"They're all crazy, Gogi. The lot of them. And speaking of crazy, have you folks been watering down the milk again?"

Gogi was taken aback. "Mrs. Reza, it is not the dairy. Oh, no. It's the weather."

"The weather?"

"Yes, expertly speaking. On these hot days, the buffaloes spend nearly all of their time in the ponds around the farm, keeping as cool as possible. That is their way. This is how the milk is naturally watered down a little."

Shez gave him a skeptical look. "You're just like your father," she said good-naturedly. "Always ready with the answers." It was the same line her father had often used on his quick-thinking little daughter.

After Gogi left, Shez drank her tea and kept watch on the alley, which was still eerily quiet. No gossips were out and about; no children were playing; there was not a happy human voice to be heard. This was not the neighborhood they had always loved. Overnight it had become another kind of place, a place she was not sure she wanted to live in.

Salman came in from the other room. "Morning, Ammi."

She smiled and nodded toward the teapot on the stove. "I just made it. They're watering down the milk again."

"That's nothing new." Salman filled a cup with the hot tea.

"Look outside."

Salman went to the window and gazed upon the alley. "Where is everyone?"

"They are afraid to show themselves, and I can't blame them. I'm afraid myself."

They sat together, mother and son, drinking their sweet-spicy tea without speaking until Shez could no longer repress a question she was afraid to ask and still more afraid to have answered. This was not a happy day, not a day for small talk.

"Sallu, your father and I are worried about Dani. After what he was saying last night . . . do you think he is in any way involved with these awful terrorists?"

Her oldest son looked at her sharply, then away.

"*Tell me*, Sallu. Is my own son a terrorist?"

"I don't know, Ammi," he said softly. "I think sometimes he is heading in that direction. He is against anything that does not advance the cause of pure religious law. That's why he did not want to stay here last night. He sees Kami as a special enemy."

Shez absorbed Salman's reply. "I ask again, do you think he's one of them?"

Salman stared into his teacup. "I do not know, Ammi. He no longer confides in me as he did when we were kids."

Shez covered her face with her hands.

Salman sprang to her side. "Please, we don't know if Dani has done anything wrong. He talks a lot and has a lot of crazy ideas he's picked up at that madrassa. But that doesn't make him a terrorist."

Shez sighed and rubbed her face.

"You know very well," Salman went on, "that young people are fed up with how things stand today. Hell, everyone is. Dani is just expressing the same disgust a lot of young people are feeling. We're all trying to cope. Don't cry, Ammi. The nation has been through troubled times before."

"Your father put his life on the line for this country."

"I know."

"He was a brave and courageous soldier. He was fighting for what he believed was right for his country."

"I know that, Ammi. I know."

Shez rubbed her reddened eyes and sniffled, muttering, "It's like they're taking it all away from him, everything he fought for."

SIX

A thousand years of blessings
can be undone by three minutes of carnage.

GEO TV NEWS CORRESPONDENT

The somewhat overdressed word "madrassa" is used throughout Pakistan and most of South Asia and refers simply to facilities devoted to the teaching of Islamic theology and religious law. Madrassas are schools, often campuslike environments of whitewashed buildings grouped around a courtyard of quiet dignity and Islamic simplicity, with a reflecting pool and spotless stone decking. Other times the local madrassa is much more humble, housed in a former warehouse or factory, and can resemble an abandoned supermarket in a Detroit slum. The madrassa that Daniyal Reza attended in Lahore was one of the smarter ones. It had been a British garrison for the Household Cavalry until World War II. The stables and barracks had been converted into classrooms and lecture halls in the 1980s. Over the next twenty years, as wars had begun to rage in Afghanistan and Iraq, enrollment at the Lahore madrassa had reached nearly 2,500, an all-time high. The madrassa was situated on a pleasant few acres in an industrial area along the outskirts of the city. The Muslim dome that had been erected above the buildings provided a touch of Arabic elegance.

For those who excelled in their religious studies, dormitory privileges were available in an adjacent hostel, a converted mansion where the garrison's commanding officer had once lived with his family, military staff, and servants. Daniyal Reza had been attending the school for six years and was an honors student in both Islamic theology and sharia law. "You are an asset to our institution, Dani," the imam had told him when he had been assigned to one of the better dorms.

The madrassa was known as the best in Lahore for traditional religious training. As Daniyal told his father, "There is no higher calling than to study the word of the Prophet, the last messenger of Allah."

"Yes," Awais had responded, "but Muhammad can be interpreted in many ways. Sometimes there are those who use the Prophet's words for their own ends. I hope you have the judgment to know the true teacher from the false teacher."

"When it comes to Islam, there are no false teachers, only false believers."

"That is where you are wrong. Wake up, Dani. The very term 'religious studies' has taken on a very sinister implication."

"That's due to Western propaganda."

"Not entirely."

Awais did not have to spell it out. Since the U.S. invasion of Afghanistan, many extremist groups had been uncovered within madrassas operating all over Pakistan. The government had shut down certain schools that were blatantly providing, as officials hazily put it, "paramilitary training." It wouldn't do to use the term "terrorist cell," to concede that insurgents were being educated and outfitted, housed and harbored under the banner of "Islamic studies." There was no doubt that most madrassas had nothing to do with terrorist operations and frequently denounced the use of violence as "counter-Islamic." Yet a small minority of madrassas went far beyond mere "paramilitary training." These were clandestine colleges of terror.

A few days after the bombing, Daniyal Reza was summoned to a private meeting with the senior imam.

Daniyal had been told that the imam wished to speak to him at 9:00 in the evening. He did not need to be told to appear promptly. At a few minutes before the appointed hour, Daniyal arrived at the mosque inside the madrassa and performed ablutions, then offered the Isha prayer, somewhat nervously.

He found his way out into the moonlit courtyard. The reflecting pool shimmered, and stars shone over Lahore like diamond chips on black velvet. The imam was the only figure in the courtyard, sitting in one of several folding chairs by the pool, drinking a green bottle of 7Up. He wore the typical bushy beard and white shift of his kind.

Daniyal went directly to him, palms pressed together. "May it please you, Imam."

The older man smiled and stood, clasping Daniyal's hands. "You please me very much and always have, Daniyal." He gestured to the folding chair next to him. "Sit. Let us talk."

Cloaked in night shadows, the imam held the stage with his silence. It was the silence of a careful man, a precise man.

Finally, quietly, the imam spoke: "My young friend, I have known you some years now. You came to us with confused ideas and misconceptions of Allah's will. And let us speak plainly: you were in some ways at war within yourself. You could not accept the ungodly morals of those English schools that infest our nation. To be blunt, you came to us with a very false interpretation of the life we have been given to live. Do you recall?"

Daniyal lowered his head and nodded.

"But that was you back then, Dani. Today you sit before me as a young man wise beyond his years. Your religious spirit is the very spirit of Islam. I shame myself with pride to believe that I have made some small contribution to your transformation."

"I am indebted to you for all that I am."

The imam fell silent again for a moment. When he finally spoke, his tone had changed, carrying a new urgency. "You are already seeing, Daniyal, that it falls to us, the true upholders of Islam, to do the hard work. To fight the fight Allah put us here to fight. Do you understand what I am saying?"

Daniyal looked at his hands. "I do."

"The offering of prayers, the fasting, observing the holy days, these are all well and good but not enough for the special kind of Muslim you were born to be. Allah has his angels for these minor duties. And we have our women to watch over things. But man is created for more exalted deeds. And there is nothing more exalted than to be an avenger for Allah. But this can only be accomplished if we, the most dedicated, do our duty." He paused to sip some 7Up. "And what is our duty, I ask you, Dani? What do we do in the face of God's enemies?"

"There is no choice. There must be jihad."

"That is the proper answer, which I expected from one of my most intelligent pupils." The imam shook his head mournfully. "These are difficult days, Dani. We have living among us not only infidels but liars, hypocrites, and pretenders. Many whom we count as neighbors, as fellow citizens, are in reality enemies. These evil ones are often seen in the disguise of the righteous and the devout.

We must see through the mask and understand that these are God's most dangerous enemies." He grimaced. "They mouth the words of the Prophet while in the pay of foreign Satans."

"I have seen this with my own eyes, Imam."

"That is because you now know *how* to see and where to look most closely. Here, in this quiet and dignified oasis devoted to God's laws, you have opened your eyes."

Daniyal lifted his head. A single tear was on his cheek.

The imam touched his arm. "Now I come to the reason for our meeting. Of course you know of our district leader, the amir Gul Nawaz?"

"Certainly, Imam. But I have not had the honor of meeting him."

"Only those he summons ever meet him. And now he is summoning you." The imam pressed Daniyal's arm. "Allah has blessed you with unique powers, my son. It is time to employ these powers in His service. Do you understand?"

"All that God wishes I shall accomplish."

The imam looked toward the starry sky. "Here in Pakistan we have many of Islam's holiest souls. We must protect them from the infidels, Dani. In Allah's name, what we did at the shrine was only the beginning."

Daniyal looked up sharply. "I am overjoyed to know that our own madrassa . . ."

"Yes. We were the instrument of retribution—the amir and his people, including the two who martyred themselves. They have shown the way, Dani. Now we must rid our country of the filth of the foreigners and their evil ways—the barbaric Western bankers, the robbers. And we must also purge their many puppets from within our own government. We must enforce sharia law at all costs." He stared into the young man's eyes. "You understand me, don't you?"

"Yes, Imam sahib."

"Then you know it is our wish and command."

Daniyal said quietly, almost in a whisper, "I am ready to do as I am commanded."

From somewhere in the folds of his shift, the bearded man produced a slip of paper and pressed it into Daniyal Reza's hand. "Go to your room. Cleanse yourself and sleep deeply. Tomorrow, right after early prayer, call this number. Allah will be with you."

∞

KAMRAN AND RANIA were in the same late-morning class on the history of the Pakistani supreme court, a subject of Byzantine intricacy, extensively dull and elaborately boring.

"You will note," the professor lectured with some private amusement, "that our supreme court is a revolving door, an endless queue of the corrupt, the sleazy, the impure, the naive. Perhaps someday, in a time far from today, we will have a true supreme court. A court that rules from a sense of justice rather than from political exigencies and undue," he rubbed his thumb over his fingers, "shall we say 'extralegal' influences?"

That drew a rippling laugh from the class.

It was all part of the learning process, and the students paid close attention to the lecture. If they were going to help lift Pakistan out of its increasingly desperate state, they had to know their way around their government, even if it put them to sleep.

After class, departing from their usual habit, Kamran and Rania went their separate ways, then met at a café off campus.

"I don't like sneaking around like this," Rania said as they sat over Turkish coffee at a back table. From the busy kitchen, snatches of a Beatles tune filtered through. "It's like they win if we knuckle under to threats from these hoodlums, which is what they are."

Kamran shrugged. "I agree. But your safety is my main concern. For now we must keep a low profile. I don't know what I might do if they harmed my precious one."

"It complicates things. I spoke to my mother."

"About us getting engaged?"

"Yes. I also told her about your encounter with that fat creep who attacked you."

"I wish you hadn't done that."

"I had to, Kam. I didn't know whom else to talk to."

"Now she'll really want you to drop me. I'm dangerous to be around."

Rania held up a hand. "We discussed that. This is the complicated part. I told her I was going to continue seeing you and that I was planning to marry you. She's still trying to talk me out of it, of course."

"Of course."

"But this time I think I got through to her. She's finally realizing that I'm a grown woman, an educated woman, more so than she. I got her to at least accept the fact that you were in my life, and I wasn't going to change that."

"And what did she say?"

"That I would need a bodyguard. And . . . I agreed to it."

Kamran looked around the café. Most of the tables were filled with young people chattering away.

"He's outside, sitting in a dark-blue Toyota. He drove me here from school. I hope you're not mad."

"Not at all. In fact, it's a good idea, Rania. I'll feel better knowing you're being protected."

"I agreed to the bodyguard, but on one condition." She sipped from the porcelain demitasse. "I insisted my mother meet with you and me."

Kamran nodded, though not enthusiastically.

"I see you love the idea. Anyway, she agreed. Now, listen, my mother is old-fashioned, you know that. In her ways, it is not correct form for you to come to our home. Not yet. We must first meet in a public venue, over tea, and have a friendly chat. We'll see how it goes from there."

"All right. If that's what you want."

"We'll meet in one of those restaurants near the campus where students and parents go. Where it's not a 'sin' to be seen together. And with my mother there, all will be proper. How does that sound?"

"Frankly, a little scary. But I guess it's time your mother and I met. Sure, let's do it."

"You'll win her over in five minutes with that charming personality of yours."

He rolled his eyes.

∽∾

IN THE DAYS immediately after the bomb attack at the shrine, as Awais had feared might happen, the retail shops in Lahore and at the Anarkali bazaar saw a drop-off in business. People were staying away from large public spaces. Police checkpoints were numerous. The TV news was full of the investigation into the suicide bombers. Scores of people had been questioned, and arrests had been made, but no one had yet been charged. The general feeling was that the government was up to its usual tricks: smoke and mirrors, putting on a big show of cracking down, while those who had masterminded the bombing had avoided scrutiny. The international reaction had been swift and predictably sympathetic. The White House had issued the usual statement offering condolences and condemning the attack. A BBC report was circulated that claimed there was evidence of official Pakistani involvement, though scant details were provided and sources went unnamed. Certain web sites known to be unfavorable toward the government were blocked, but this was claimed to be a technical glitch and not an act of censorship. Nobody believed it.

Salman Reza entered his father's shop in the Anarkali bazaar a good while before he was scheduled to take his shift. His father was occupied with replacing a battery in a customer's wristwatch. Salman went into the back and poured himself a cup of cold tea. When Awais finished with the customer, he joined his son. "Don't ask how bad business is, Sallu. It's all of these street checkpoints that are keeping people from going out."

"I had to show my ID twice just walking from home."

"You're early. Something wrong?"

"Abba, I'm worried about Mother."

"How so?"

"I had a talk with her the other day and again a little while ago. She's upset. She's afraid Dani could be involved with terrorists at his madrassa—might even be involved in the killings at the shrine. Does she have any proof? No, nothing at all. It's just another of her 'premonitions,' Abba."

"I know. We talked about it. Don't turn up your nose at her premonitions. The woman is positively psychic. You remember how the army told her I had been killed in Bangladesh? She had it from official sources but refused to accept it. She told me she just 'knew' I was still alive. As for Dani, we all know his sympathies are with the extremists. Of course Ammi is worried. So am I."

"I don't know," Salman said. "Do you really think little Dani would go out and actually kill people? I find that hard to believe. He's got a head full of ideas, but it's all talk."

"Let us hope so."

Awais eased himself down into a chair. He was feeling his age, and it was showing. Gone was the wiry strength of the hard-fighting lance corporal, replaced by the heavily laden features of a prematurely aged man, a man who had not been happy for years. He kept to his sunset prayers but sometimes could not make it to the morning devotion. Never a strictly religious man, he stayed as close to God as he could, but in his own way.

"We Rezas are honest people who mean no harm to anyone. You have even heard me praise Hindus, Christians, and Jews on many occasions. Whatever hatred Dani holds in his heart came from outside our family."

"My brother a terrorist. I don't buy it."

"I'm not so sure. But listen closely, Sallu. There is something I must tell you. Maybe this has something to do with Dani, or maybe it has nothing to do with him. Whatever the case may be, over the last few days I have noticed a man loitering around. I think he's watching the shop and maybe the house too. He looks like he could be a policeman."

"A policeman? Why would the police be spying on us?"

Awais nodded. "Yes, why would they? Who knows, maybe it's all part of this phony hunt for suspects in the bombing. Let me ask you, what did Kamran say about this man who threatened him at school? He wouldn't tell me much."

"He said he was accosted by a guy who gave him a stern warning about mixing with females. Going against Islamic law and all that. You know, the same old crap."

"Yes, the same line Dani spouts. Think about it . . . the authorities are hunting down extremists. At the very same time, we suddenly have someone spying on us. Could Dani have attracted their attention?"

"But there are thousands who think like him all over Lahore, Abba. Why would he be singled out?"

"This is also my question."

THAT DAY AFTER morning prayer, Daniyal Reza called the phone number the imam had given him. He was instructed to leave his dorm with just a few personal items in a plain shopping bag, not a suitcase. If anyone asked, he was to say he was off to a family outing. But he simply avoided talking to anyone and went to the designated corner at the time he'd been given. Soon an old Peugeot sedan picked him up and drove north into the suburbs, taking a circuitous route that avoided police checkpoints. The young driver said not a word, and Daniyal kept to himself.

Forty-five minutes later, the car turned into the driveway of a large three-story colonial house on a dead-end street. Behind the building, the driveway opened up into a wide central court. Several vehicles and motor scooters were parked in front of the four-car garage. This was one of the Pakistani Taliban's fancier safe houses.

Daniyal was shown to an austere room on the top floor. A large poster over the sleeping mat quoted verses from religious text and sermons of popular religious leaders. Within the hour, another silent young man brought Daniyal a fine meal of steamed rice and braised lamb. Afterward he took out his scriptures and sat at the little desk, reading intently. Periodically he erupted with words of prayer or praise, as was his habit when especially moved by the holy text.

A little before evening prayers, the powerful amir, Gul Nawaz, came to see him, all smiles and compliments. "Welcome, Daniyal. You honor us with your presence here. The imam has told me all about your learning. I am most impressed."

"I take no credit for myself, Amir."

"You are one of Allah's special servants. Why do I say this? Because you have seen the true light and have grasped the meaning of it all." Nawaz was the regional strongman, the final voice on all operational matters. He was middle-aged, healthy and stout, his beard trim, his longish hair center-parted. The simple cotton kurtha he wore was unbuttoned, revealing a long scar across his breast. His left eye was lazy, and it gave him a slightly threatening squint, as though he were a little deranged. "Come with me, Dani. We have our own mosque."

After their devotions, Nawaz took Daniyal into a large carpeted room shut off by double doors. They sat on mats and were served by yet another silent young man, who brought them tea and hashish-laced cigarettes. Nawaz made a ceremony out of lighting up the hashish and passing it to Daniyal. Within a short time, a drug-induced clarity took over, and Daniyal was receptive to all the amir had to tell him.

"This is the ancient tradition of the *hassassin* and goes back to the time of the Crusades." He shrugged. "At least that was thought to be the story until some clever scholar came along recently and claimed that the devotees did not use hashish. Still, I find it helps in our special work. How do you feel?"

"At one with myself."

"You know, Dani, our country stands to lose all we have achieved since our independence from the English infidels and the evil rulers of India. We have a government that takes its orders from abroad. We are losing our country. Allah is not pleased. They have tried various forms of unholy government, so-called democratic government, where little attention is paid to the demands of Islam. Of course they have not worked and never will. It is as true now as it always has been—the only way Pakistan can be saved is through the glory and truth of Islam. This means a strict application of sharia law everywhere in the nation. This is something you understand very well, Dani."

"That is so, Amir."

"And what is sharia law?"

Daniyal took his time answering. "Sharia is the infallible law of Allah applied to daily life. It is separate and above the laws of man."

"Very good. Sharia is God's law, and man must follow that law above his own or be damned for eternity." The amir's left eye drifted as he took several deep puffs from the hashish cigarette and then passed it to Daniyal. "You are soon to have a glorious reward for your dedication to Allah's will."

"All I am belongs to God. Any rewards are of no concern."

Nawaz was warming to his subject. "The infidels are too ignorant to conceive of the majestic place we call heaven. Many do not believe in an afterlife. They say that when we die, we go to the same place we were before we were born. This is the poverty of imagination that is rampant in the West. Upon their heads we must bring jihad. Are you ready to strike to secure God's domain?"

The hashish high showed in Daniyal's face, red and intense. "I have always been ready to serve, Amir. It is the fate Allah has marked out for me since birth."

Gul Nawaz extracted a sheet of paper from a folder and gave it to Daniyal. "Here are your farewell words. Please commit them to memory." He looked at his watch. "We can shoot the video as soon as you're ready."

∞

AWAIS AND SHEZ had a quiet dinner at home, as most people in metropolitan Lahore were doing. The police checkpoints had now been supplemented by army roadblocks. Anyone out on the street after dark was subject to being stopped and searched. A minor infraction could result in an arrest, which could lead to a death sentence. Even during more ordinary times, people had a way of disappearing into thin air in Pakistan, but the security crackdown after the bombing at the shrine had made the situation worse.

"If this emergency period keeps up," Awais said over his vegetable stew, "we'll all go broke at the bazaar. Everyone is down a good 50 percent in the last few days."

"That man was hanging around in the alley again," Shez said. "You know, the dark-skinned one you saw outside the shop."

"I saw a different one today, a younger man. He was pretending to buy from the produce stalls across the way. There's no doubt they're watching us."

Shez sat back, losing interest in the food. "You probably think I'm dwelling on the worst of our fears. But I have this strong sensation that Dani is . . . that they're looking for him. But where is he? Why don't you call his hostel, Awais? See if he's there."

He shook his head. "No, that will only draw attention to him. If something is going on with Dani, we need to stay completely out of it."

"In the name of Allah!" Shez burst out. "What has happened to our family?"

Awais took his wife's hand. "It's the times we live in, dear one. We must face it. Instead of the pleasant and peaceful existence we could have had, Pakistan has become a war zone, and we're the refugees."

Shez looked out the window, wistful, thoughtful. "There must be a better world somewhere," she murmured.

SEVEN

So he who does an atom's weight of good will see it,
and he who does an atom's weight of evil will see it.

AL-QURAN

A day came when the Reza family no longer felt able to call itself "middle class." Other than the house in Lahore and the shop in the Anarkali bazaar, they owned nothing substantial—no land, no valuables. Awais had been successful in his trade, but since the terror wars had begun in the new century, he was, like all the merchant class, under constant economic stress. Profits were often eaten up by the bribes that had to be paid whether business was good or bad. Kamran was able to attend law school only by scoring high on a test for the few scholarship spots available to economically needy students. He had undertaken a two-month nonstop study marathon, and it paid off.

Kamran understood very well that the scholarship gave him a rare opportunity to rise above his family's station in life. He was determined not to fail himself or his family. He went to class with gusto and a keen eye for the important, the essential. He was prepared and attentive. He worked hard and earned top grades while garnering more than his share of compliments from the professors. At first, being around classmates who came from money and had important family connections, Kamran naturally felt more than a little outclassed, even an outsider. But over time, his high academic achievements and the confidence he gained in his relationship with Rania gave him a certain status within the close-knit student community. He was the bright boy from Anarkali, admired and respected by faculty and students alike.

When word got around that Kamran had been confronted and assaulted by an Islamist over his public association with Rania, the matter was brought up for discussion in class.

"This unfortunate episode provides us with a perfect illustration," Professor Qasim lectured, "of the basic situation we face in Pakistan today. On one hand, we have the devout Islamic followers who strive to dictate how we should all live. On the other hand, we have the better educated who seek a more pluralistic, more democratic society—to throw off the shackles of ancient prejudice and superstition and live in the modern world. Make no mistake about it, students: within Pakistan, a great race is now being run. Quote: 'a race between education and catastrophe.'" He looked around the classroom. "Whom am I quoting? Come, now, anyone?" He shook his head sadly. "Nobody reads H. G. Wells anymore?"

The students fell to scribbling in their notebooks and tapping their smart phones.

"The point is, the contrast is clear. Our dear classmates Kami and Rania sit here today representing the new and better-educated

Pakistan, while this self-righteous gentleman who sees fit to rudely instruct us in Islamic proprieties represents the Pakistan of yesterday's notions, outdated systems, and discarded lies. However, take note. The extremists have a powerful weapon we do not possess. And that weapon is? . . ."

"Violence," several students called out.

"Yes, but not just violence. Violence perpetrated *in the name of God*. They say God tells them to kill. And it is by the use of this 'divinely sanctioned' bloodshed that they hope to terrorize us into accepting their Islamic brand of theocratic rule. God wants it, so you'd better do it, or else. They come on like the villains in a James Bond movie. They want to rule the world. The question we have considered many times in this class is more critical now than ever before: Are these scare tactics working? Will the great mass of people knuckle under and allow the extremists to take control? Whether out of fear or belief, which can be the same thing."

It was a major theme of Professor Qasim's class and one of the nation's most pressing and complex issues, as important as the debate about Pakistan's moribund economy: What should be done about the militants operating within Pakistan? The alliance with the United States was not helping the situation on the ground or in the arena of public opinion. The national cooperation with Washington was now openly questioned by everyone from the media to the man on the street.

"Is Islam itself to blame?" the professor queried. "Remember that Islam is at heart a caring, a forgiving, religion."

"Yes, Professor, but it is a religion that can and should be criticized," a student pointed out, "for its intolerance and calls to warfare."

"All religions are intolerant," another student declared.

"And full of excesses."

Rania jumped into the discussion. "It is not Islam we should blame. It is the way certain people of questionable goodness use religion as a weapon to gain control over the masses. It's really an old, old story and is found in cultures throughout history. Religion itself scares people and can be a powerful tool of oppression and intimidation."

Professor Qasim was pleased. "Very good, Rania. What you say is quite true. Religion stirs the blood and makes people feel they have the right to force their views on others. A moment ago, I quoted an English author. Let's stay in the West and quote the American civil rights leader Malcolm X, himself a Muslim. He said, I think rather wisely, 'Do everyone a favor. Leave your religion at home.' If that were universally applied, we would all be better off. Anyone disagree?"

ﻌ

MUCH OF THE television news was centered around the counter-terrorist campaign that had spread from Lahore to other cities. The government was acting as if the outrage at the shrine had been some kind of last straw and was now earnestly rooting out terror cells. In fact, as everyone very well knew, it had been prompted to action by the threat of losing billions in aid from Washington. More than one high-profile U.S. lawmaker was calling for a nonpartisan investigation into Pakistan's use of foreign aid. In news clips seen and heard around the world, a member of the House Committee on Ways and Means made it clear that he thought the United States was being played for a sucker. "Let's get real," he said in one clip, "Pakistan pretends to be on our side just to get that American dollar. They're not against terrorism; they're involved in it themselves. I think it's high time we stopped shoveling greenbacks at these false friends."

These high-flown matters of state were of no concern to Daniyal Reza. Indeed, very little of this world was now his concern. He was focused only on his fate and the final service he would render. The whole idea of what he was going to do gave him an intense, rapturous sense of honor and pride, while the hashish he smoked provided visions of Allah's promises beyond earthly bounds. "The glory, the *glory*," he would whisper at prayer.

Daniyal had been joined at the safe house first by one young man and then by a second, Nasir and Raj. In just a couple of days, a unique closeness had developed between the three of them, the bond of infinity. They would martyr themselves and forever after rejoice in Allah's presence. The amir had not yet informed them of the details of the plan, but they knew it would be an important blow against the godless, the defiled, and the profane.

"You are the frontline soldiers," Gul Nawaz declared. "You are the brave shock troops whom Allah has chosen to wage jihad, to battle the infidels—here, at this time, in this place. You will destroy them for His utmost glory."

Daniyal and the other two were so overcome with emotion that they could not speak. They gripped each other's hands and lowered their heads, shamed by their own insignificance and their part in the Great Immensity.

Among the three boys, Raj held a special prestige and place of distinction because his older brother had been one of the two martyrs responsible for the sacred triumph at the shrine. Raj was deferred to, listened to, and at mealtimes given first choice from the common plates, though he always declined and humbly took his portion last. The three of them did not laugh very often or engage in the kind of joshing usually seen in a tight-knit group of young men. They were ultraholy men hell-bent on pleasing God in heaven; there was little time left for pleasantries.

"Our time in paradise is coming," Raj said to the other two. "Let us promise to meet there in that land, where we shall all live forever."

Their hearts were joined in brotherhood. Keeping their spirits in the right place, they each read selected passages aloud from the hadith books, the teachings and sayings of Muhammad. Daniyal chose to repeat only one line over and over: "Fight them until all opposition ends and all submit to Allah." He looked up and repeated, "Fight them until *all* submit to Allah. These are the Last Messenger's words."

That night after prayer, Gul Nawaz took them out to the garage behind the house. Motor scooters were parked next to the old Peugeot that had brought each of them to the safe house. "Do any of you know how to drive one of these machines?" Navaz asked, indicating the scooters.

They each had a smattering of experience on scooters, but none were very skilled.

One of the quiet serving men came out, and the lights in the courtyard were turned on. The man instructed the three honored ones in how to drive a scooter. "Once you try it a few times, it's as easy as riding a bicycle."

∞

THE KNOCK ON the Reza family's door in Anarkali came late at night. It was not the knock of a neighbor needing assistance or the knock of a family member looking for shelter or the timid knock of the helpless begging for a handout. It was the unignorable knock of authority.

Awais was not yet in bed, though Shez was almost asleep. The knocking brought her instantly awake. "Who is it, Awais?"

"I'll find out. Stay in bed and let me handle this."

"I told you, Awais; we are marked, and there will be trouble."

"Do not worry, my dear. Go back to sleep."

"How can I sleep?"

Awais went into the living room and opened the front door.

A man in a plain shirt and tie held up an ID card. "Good evening. My name is Jamaz, and I'm a sergeant with the local constabulary, Mr. Reza. I'm sorry to bother you at this hour, but I need a few words with you, if I may."

"Very well." Awais stepped out onto the landing, closed the door behind him, and stood in the deep shadows with the officer. The nightly power cuts were still in effect, and there was no electric lighting. "Please speak quietly. My neighbors are sleeping. What can I do for you, Sergeant?"

"Is Daniyal Reza your son?"

"Yes."

"Do you know where we can find him?"

"He stays at a hostel in Lahore."

"Yes, we've searched his room. Daniyal has not been there for days. This is a serious matter, Mr. Reza. I realize he is your son, but if you know where he is, you must tell me. It is the law."

Awais was not intimidated. He'd long ago passed the point where a policeman could frighten him. "I have seen you and another man watching my shop in the bazaar and our house. So you certainly know that Dani hardly ever comes to see us. Why are you looking for my son? What has he done?"

"I'm not at liberty to say, Mr. Reza. Do you know the imam at his madrassa?"

"I have only heard Dani speak of him."

"It might interest you to know that the imam has been arrested, along with some of his followers. The madrassa has been shut down. Daniyal was last seen there in the company of the imam."

Awais shrugged. "I know nothing of his whereabouts. He seldom calls, and we have no idea what he is doing these days. He is a good person and follows the strictures of the holy word."

"Yes, we understand that he has been well trained in religious matters." The sergeant paused. "You must understand, we will have to take you into custody if you do not tell the truth, Mr. Reza."

"The truth has been spoken. I cannot tell you where my son is. I simply don't know."

"Let me accept that for now as the truth. But I want your word that if you hear from Daniyal or learn his whereabouts, you will let us know. I want your promise."

Awais shook his head. "I cannot make such a promise. Turn my own son in to the authorities? That I will not do. I will not do your work for you. You might as well take me to jail right now."

The officer watched Awais's lined and unyielding face. He finally broke into a half smile and patted Awais on the shoulder. "Very well, old soldier. At least you're being honest about that. It tells me you are likely being truthful with the rest of it. I won't keep you any longer, Mr. Reza. Good evening."

"Good evening, sir."

When Awais went back inside, he found Shez sitting up in bed, tense and anxious. "It was the police, wasn't it?"

"Yes. You were right. They're looking for Dani. For what reason, he would not tell."

Shez fixed her husband with a soulful stare. "Even terrorists have parents," she mumbled distractedly. "We have to try to find Dani."

"There's no way we can do that. We don't have the contacts that would help us find him. Besides, they're watching us, remember. We could end up leading the police right to him. And then we'd be implicated too. No, we will not look for Dani."

Shez said, "I keep asking myself, what did we do wrong? He was a sweet child and always listened to his parents."

"You're more religious than I am, Shez, so you'd know more about this. But don't you see, it's that madrassa he's been attending. He was a young and impressionable kid. This mullah and his disciples have no doubt filled his head with all of these extreme views. That's where Dani went wrong, not here at home. We always respected Islam, but never did we suggest that violence is part of it."

"Islam is not about violence," Shez said firmly.

"My dear lady, religion can be used to make people do anything."

∞

LIKE MOST PEOPLE, Awais Reza understood the national mood very well. It was becoming increasingly grim and erratic. In the months leading up to the shrine bombing, there had been three or four suicide attacks around Pakistan every week. Some of these were clumsy, low-wattage missions: a would-be martyr outside Karachi blew himself and his car into metal and bone fragments as he was trying to reach a motorcade of VIPs. Except for the bomber, no one was hurt. Other times, the hate-fueled killers were astonishingly bloodthirsty. In an exclusive suburb south of Islamabad, a suicide bomber posed as a kitchen helper at a country club. He placed twenty pounds of Semtex in the pan of an aluminum serving cart. Slipping on a waiter's jacket, he rolled the cart into the dining area crowded with bankers, businessmen, and merchants out for a family dinner. When he reached the center of the room, he lifted a wire and screamed something about God. The blast brought down the building, killing forty and injuring more than a hundred. This was the thunderous rumble of encroaching violence that was daily in the back of Awais's mind, an ever-present tremor of fear. "Every day I wake up and wonder what's next," he confided to another shop owner at the bazaar.

The frequent and unpredictable attacks were especially hard on the teenagers and young people such as Kamran and his class. As they were reaching adulthood, it was soul-destroying to see the country convulsed by violent upheavals. Some 60 percent of Pakistan's population had been under the age of twenty-five for the first decade of the new century, a generation of the concerned and the fretful. It seemed that each day the news brought more frightening evidence of the future they were all heading toward and would have to live in. Rania observed in class one day that bombings and shootings had become so commonplace that they were almost an accepted fact of life.

"Has anyone noticed? Unless there is some major incident, people don't seem to take much notice anymore. As a society, we're getting too comfortable coexisting with the extremists."

It was a point the class readily acknowledged. While facing an uncertain future, those in school, like young people everywhere across the country, had to cope with a split-personality life, an emotional balancing act between the rigorous demands of Muslim family life and the seductive imports and technological innovations of the progressive West. They were not only a worried generation, they were also a hemmed-in generation. Young educated Pakistanis such as Kamran Reza knew they would fall hopelessly behind in the emerging global economy if they did not embrace the modern world. Yet some Muslim traditions (as they were commonly practiced), Muslim identity, forbade any such alliance. The young lived in a world where much of their social life had to be hidden. They liked Hollywood films, rock music, and modern dancing, but these were simply not acceptable and could be indulged only at some risk. Certainly the revealing clothing so fashionable in godless places such as New York was completely out of the question. A trip to McDonald's or Kentucky Fried Chicken could bring a stern lecture or even severe punishment. Western-style dating was still widely considered vulgar and unclean, an insult to Islamic code. Violating the strictures against unmarried male-female pairing often resulted in murderous assaults and grotesque maimings. Courts were typically lenient toward the perpetrators of such crimes, considering religious beliefs to be mitigating circumstances.

The social constraints alienated many youths, and some became exactly the type of young person that the extremists sought
to recruit: those without hope. Many young recruits came from rea-
sonably well-to-do families, not just those in poverty and in need.
Disaffection is a powerful force.

The ancient custom of arranged marriages is widespread in
Pakistan, as in much of the subcontinent. Within the culture, marriage is a financial and social transaction, and honor and family ex-
pectations are central to the process. Fathers are always looking to
marry a daughter to a wealthy man, and they display a bank-book
directness seldom seen in polite Western society. For traditional
Pakistani families, the idea of love being the sole criterion in se-
lecting a marriage partner seems like a Western-style gimmick.
Nonetheless, the younger generation overwhelmingly wants to
choose a partner on the basis of emotional and psychological com-
patibility. As Rania told Kamran, "Women are different today. We
need to control our own lives, and that includes whom we marry."
Over time, the tradition of the arranged marriage will begin to
fade—but it will not fade quickly.

∽

SALMAN WAS TENDING the shop in the Anarkali bazaar when
Kamran came in. "I caught a ride with Zain. I can't stay long."

Salman took him into the back for some tea from the cooler. "I
guess you heard," Salman said, filling paper cups.

"Yes, Abba called me. The police are looking for Dani. However,
I ask you, is that any big shock?"

Salman shook his head in dismay. "I don't know. They still
haven't said he's done anything wrong. Just that they want to talk to
him."

"Uh-huh, talk to him. How are Abba and Ammi taking it?"

"Not well. He didn't even want to come in to the shop this morning. She had to talk him into it. He hasn't missed a day in years."

"So they've had a surveillance team watching the shop and the house," Kamran said. "Is it still going on?"

Salman stepped to the back window and drew the curtain aside a couple of inches to peer out. "Yes, he's still there. One in front too. They carry guns, you know."

Kamran sat down and drank the tea. "It's that madrassa. They've rounded up the whole lot of them. I knew it would come to this. Let's be blunt: Dani's involved with a terror cell. People like him are being arrested all over Pakistan."

"How do we know Dani has done anything? They could be questioning everybody who went to the madrassa. Going to a religious school is not a crime."

"It can be," Kamran muttered.

Salman put a hand on his brother's shoulder. "If something does happen . . . and Dani is involved in . . . well, whatever, will that hurt you at school?"

"Hurt me? They'll probably cancel my scholarship. I'll never be able to get into another law school. And of course Rania's parents will pull the plug on any engagement. Yes, if Dani gets into the kind of trouble I think he's in, it'll hurt me, you, our whole family. Abba could even lose this shop. Speaking of which, how's business?"

Salman threw up his hands. "What business? Who wants to come to the bazaar these days? When police are on the street, people get nervous and stay home."

Kamran stood. "I have to meet Zain for a ride back to school. I must not miss sunset prayers this evening. I have much to ask of Allah."

Their parting hug was firm. "I remember when you were very

little," Salman recalled, "always whining for sweets. Well guess what I've got for you? Your favorite candy bar."

"Hershey's?"

"I took in half a case this afternoon. My smuggler gave me a deal."

"The jumbo ones or the regular size?"

Salman laughed. "The big ones, of course. I have four set aside for you."

After Kamran left with his contraband chocolate bars, Salman brought out a minipipe and a nugget of opium he'd bought from the confectioner's deliveryman. He pulled the blinds closed in the front and sat down in back. He needed something to calm himself.

∞

DESPITE THE DREADFUL times for the country and the mounting crisis within the family, Shez had gone back to her work at the hospital on the outskirts of Anarkali. Awais had not objected. He knew she felt good helping others, using her training, and keeping up her practical nursing skills. But now things were different, and it was not safe to go out at night. "Can't you do your shift during the day?" Awais complained.

"There are plenty of qualified nurses for the daytime. It is the evening shift that is hard to staff for the nurses' station. They depend on me, Awais. The wards are full of patients from the bombing. Besides, it's only two nights a week, and we have secure transportation."

The terrorists had made public threats against the medical personnel who were treating the victims of the bombing. The hospital had issued special ID badges for getting quickly through security checkpoints. Unmarked vans were being used to pick up workers at their homes and deliver them to the hospital. An army officer sat in the front passenger seat, a machine gun across his lap. The same procedure was used for returning the nurses home once their shifts had ended.

Shez had been shocked at the injuries from the bombing and had worked with hardly a break to comfort and treat her patients. She had her own problems, but before her were those who were far worse off and needed her immediate care. One issue quickly became critical: with the sudden intake of so many badly injured victims, the hospital's resources were rapidly being drained. Already they were out of certain drugs and were in danger of depleting their supply of even basic medications.

"You can blame our wonderful government," the head nurse confided to Shez. "We were given a sizable grant last year, but has anyone seen a rupee of it? The whole damn thing was nothing but a photo op for that fool Zardari and his people."

"We have received none of the money?" Shez asked.

"None of it," the older nurse snapped. She dropped her voice. "You can bet those private hospitals aren't running short of anything." She went down to a whisper. "And you can bet certain government people have our money sitting in their foreign bank accounts right now. You can bet on that. Meanwhile, we're running out of sterile bandages."

EIGHT

With faith, discipline and selfless devotion to duty,
there is nothing worthwhile that you cannot achieve.
MOHAMMED ALI JINNAH, QUAID-E-AZAM

The angels of death awoke early and made their beds.

It was still dark outside when the three young men assembled in the breakfast room, where they were served meat pastries, goat's milk, and tea. Presently Gul Nawaz made his appearance. He was in the uniform of a major in the Pakistani army, complete with a heavy-caliber sidearm.

"Sometimes we join the infidels to defeat them," he explained. "My honorable ones, we are moving to another safe house. This is strictly a routine precaution. The entire government has been thrown into turmoil by our glorious achievement at the shrine. They are running around like fools, making a big show of arresting religious leaders. One of these is our own imam. He does not know our current location and would not disclose it even if he did. But your holy mission is far too important to take risks."

The transfer would normally be risky. With all of the police and military patrols on the street, any civilian vehicle could be stopped at any time. But Gul Nawaz was adept at countersecurity measures and had frequently adopted the "false flag" tactic. With a single phone call to a "grocer," using a certain code phrase in his food order, he had summoned an authentic Pakistani military van, now parked in the courtyard. Daniyal, Raj, and Nasir would play the part of detainees, men already in army custody.

"If we run into a random roadblock, there will be no question of interfering with an officer who has prisoners in tow." Nawaz grinned and slapped his leather holster, the lazy eye menacing. "You see, we outsmart them each step of the way."

∞

KAMRAN AND RANIA met at another out-of-the-way tea shop far from the campus. It was becoming their routine—leaving class separately, meeting clandestinely, with Rania's armed bodyguard nearby in the Toyota sedan.

They settled at a table in back. The serving girl took their order for strong tea and cinnamon crisps. "We have to give my mother a date for our meeting," Rania said. "She will need to see her hairdresser and all that just before. I'm afraid she's somewhat vain."

"I hate to tell you this, Rania, but look . . . we might want to put off getting together with your mother. At least for a while."

"You've changed your mind about meeting her?"

"Of course not. I want to meet both of your parents. It's . . . something else."

"I'm listening."

The tea arrived, and Kamran drank while gathering his thoughts. "I've told you about my brother Dani."

"I know, he's the fanatic in the family."

"Yes, and now he's in trouble. He's apparently mixed up in something at the madrassa he belongs to in Lahore. The police are looking for him."

She sagged. "Oh, no."

"I'm sorry about this. We don't know what it's all about, but they've been watching the store at the bazaar and the house too. A policeman came to talk to my father. They've searched Dani's hostel. They've arrested the imam and his people."

Rania sat twisting her hands.

"It might be that they want him only for questioning about the imam," Kamran said. "Right now we don't know what Dani may or may not have done." He could barely look at the girl across the table. "Rania, we should wait on our engagement."

She sat up, her back rigid. "No. We're already forced to sneak around, and now we have to give up our plans for the future? *No.*"

"Just until we see how this situation develops. Be practical, Rania. Your father is an important man in the government. He would never allow his daughter to marry into the family of a terrorist."

Rania leaned across the table. "You said yourself, we don't know why the police are looking for Dani. They are arresting a lot of people these days. And so what if he is arrested? That is no indication of guilt. We still have some semblance of law in this country."

"I wouldn't count on that." Kamran started to munch on a crisp, then put it back on the plate. "We're all hoping that his offense, if any, is something small." He fixed her with a steady gaze. "But I have to be honest for your sake." He lowered his voice. "I don't think it is something small. Remember how he's always gone off on those 'pilgrimages' with the madrassa?"

"Many religious people go on those trips."

"I know. But it would also be a perfect cover story. Maybe they're not going on these religious recruiting drives, like they say. Maybe they're going back into those hidden camps in the mountains. The Pakistani Taliban are all over there. I think Dani has . . . " He fell silent a moment while the serving girl refilled their teacups. "I think he's gone all the way. That's just my feeling. I've heard him talk about what happened at the shrine. He claims it was consecrated by God."

Rania lowered her voice but spit out her words. "Damn it. Are we going to let the hooligans rule us, run our lives? Tell us what we can and cannot do?"

"Isn't that the question everyone is asking these days?"

"I'm not talking about everyone, Kam. I'm being selfish. I'm thinking of you and me. Are we going to let this crazy world stop our engagement? I say no—*hell* no."

Kamran drank some tea and sat thinking a moment. "Okay, you're right. So they're looking for my brother. That's no reason I should ask you to alter your plans, our plans." He smiled sheepishly. "I'm looking forward to meeting your mother. I'll be nervous, but I'll try some of that charm you were talking about."

She was watching his eyes and seemed to be lost in them. "We'll have a happy life together, Kam. We belong together."

"You're pretty charming yourself, young lady. In fact, so charming, I've gone to great trouble to smuggle in some of your favorite Western treats. When was the last time you had a Hershey bar?"

Rania smiled with delight. "You certainly know how to please a lady, don't you, young man?"

∞

WHEN AWAIS GOT HOME in the late afternoon, he looked tired, a sadder version of his normally upbeat self. His typical greeting was not as warm as usual. Shez already had the doodh patti tea on the stove. She stood in the kitchen doorway as her husband slumped on the couch, not bothering to snap on the TV set.

"Have you heard anything more?"

Awais shook his head. "No. I even called the madrassa. No one answers the phone. Just a recording saying the school is temporarily closed."

"They still have someone watching us. He's across the street now."

"I saw him. They're still watching the shop too. I expect it will continue until Dani surfaces." He picked up the remote control. "The news is coming on soon. I'm almost afraid to watch."

"If Dani is arrested, will they let us know?"

Awais shrugged. "That's a good question. I could phone that sergeant who came to the door. He seemed a decent enough chap. He might be able to tell us something."

"It's this waiting and not knowing . . . "

When the milk tea was ready, they sat together on the couch and sipped the soothing brew.

"Awais, we need to have a Quran khwani, a full recitation, here in our home. We must pray for our family's well-being."

He nodded, wearily, a mixture of acceptance and resignation.

"I talked to Sallu," she said hesitantly. "He talked to Kami. Well . . . this is awful, but Kami thinks he could lose his scholarship if Dani is found to be mixed up with the terrorists."

Awais lifted a hand and dropped it limply. "We don't know if Dani will even be charged with anything." He gazed at his wife. "What do your senses tell you?"

She lowered her head, palms together, whispered a few words of prayer, then looked up. "I've already said, I sense we are all heading for trouble."

"Anything is possible these days." He let out a long sigh. "It's Kami that I'm most worried about. That boy has worked long and hard to become a lawyer. We all stand to benefit. But if that is taken away . . . " He shook his head in dismay. "All my life I've known violence and bloodshed. I have always hoped to see an end to it. I realize now it will not end in the years I have left. These are cursed times, Shez. We live in bad times. Long ago was better. Look at this man Zardari we have as a president. He is the most ineffectual leader we've ever had. A complete disaster. He's just another thief."

∞

AT THE ANARKALI BAZAAR, business was still slack, though there were signs the citizenry was getting used to the security clampdown, the random stops, the ID checks, the frisking. After all, Pakistan had gone through so many "emergencies" that people were almost immune to being pushed around.

Salman Reza had a customer that afternoon who bought an emerald-set bracelet for his wife's birthday. That put a decent number of rupees in the till.

After the customer had been thanked and blessed and sent on his way with still more blessings, Salman stepped out into the bright sunshine and looked around. Here and there were groups of women shopping, keeping close together as they picked over produce and game hens. Perhaps business was slowly coming back. Salman had seen it before: some dreadful violence was perpetrated, an emergency was declared, and people stayed home for a while. But they always came back eventually to the Anarkali bazaar.

He took note of the middle-aged man in a cotton smock who was loitering in an alleyway. He'd been in and out of there for hours, keeping an eye on everything. Just ignore him, Abba had instructed.

Salman went back inside and busied himself with arranging bolts of cloth on the side tables. Once he was satisfied with a pleasing display with the richest shades on top, he went into the back and took out the opium pipe for a quick puff or two. These were stressful days.

Abruptly there came a loud bang, then a second. The unmistakable sound of gunshots.

Salman rushed to the front of the shop and looked out. A man in a flowing robe was running past the store. The middle-aged man who'd been on surveillance duty staggered out of the alley, blood seeping through the front of his smock. He stood unsteadily, raised his pistol, and let loose a barrage of shots—three, four, five rounds. He stumbled forward a few steps, dropped the gun, and fell.

Salman ran out into the narrow street. To his left, the man in the flowing robe was sprawled faceup on a collapsed clothing rack. To Salman's right, the policeman was lying in the gutter, a pool of blood running out from under him. Shop owners and customers were coming out into the street. Salman stood transfixed by the vivid evidence of death at his very doorstep.

Now he looked at the dead man in the flowing robe. He walked a few steps closer until he could see the man's open-eyed face staring skyward. Salman stepped even closer for a clear look. "No," he muttered and ran back into the store.

∞

KAMRAN WAS IN HIS DORMITORY at school, making a halfhearted attempt to get through some dry text on the screen of his hand-me-down laptop. He had parted with Rania on a good note, but an uneasy feeling about Daniyal lingered, disturbing his study time. When Zain came in from the hallway, Kamran gladly took a break.

"Right now," Zain said, "it's just a rumor, but word is the authorities are going to launch a crackdown on the colleges and universities. We're supposed to be fomenting unrest with our crazy 'radical' ideas."

"We are," Kamran said, "but it's the kind of unrest this country needs." He swung around in his chair, ready to talk ideas, a great diversion for the depressed. "We have two big problems, and one feeds on the other—corruption and terrorism. The whole *rishwa* system, the constant bribery we see every day. The extremists point to these 'immoral' activities as an indication of how society is decaying in a democratic system. A pure Islamic state, they argue, would not permit corruption. If you care to buy that line."

"Under the right Islamic leadership," Zain said, "corruption would be all but eliminated. It would go against Allah's ways to bribe and cheat. It simply wouldn't be done or permitted."

Kamran almost laughed. "You'd better go back and study human nature. Even God can't make everyone perfect."

"A faithful Islamic regime would never allow what goes on now. Look at the National Assembly. The average annual salary is something like $15,000. But we have seen the study that shows that the declared assets of nearly every assembly member is close to $1 million U.S. And this when three-quarters of Pakistanis exist on $2 a day. One member's assets are said to be 3.2 *billion* rupees! There is no way an official can accumulate that kind of wealth honestly. The current system is rotten to the core, and the Islamic model would be a definite improvement."

"It would be a step backward," Kamran insisted.

When his cell phone rang, Kamran looked at the caller ID. "It's Abba; I'd better take this," he said, and Zain politely slipped out of the room. "Yes, Abba, what is it?"

"Kami," his father answered, "there's been a shooting in front of the store."

"What?"

"I just got off the phone with Sallu. You know that policeman who has been watching the store for days now?"

"Yes, Sallu told me about the surveillance."

"Well, he was shot," Awais said. "Sallu saw it happen. The policeman was shot, but he managed to shoot back at the gunman. They're both dead."

"But why would anyone—"

"Listen, Kami. Sallu recognized the man who shot the policeman. He was a friend of Dani's."

Kamran slumped in his chair.

"Dani brought him to the shop one day, and Sallu talked to him briefly. They might try to blame this on us," Awais said. "You could well get a visit from the authorities. Just tell them the truth—that you know nothing about your brother's activities or those of his friends."

∞

GUL NAWAZ HAD ENGINEERED a smooth transition from safe house to safe house in the military van. With Nawaz in the uniform of a Pakistani army major and Daniyal, Raj, and Nasir sitting like prisoners behind a screened-off backseat, it had been simple to pass through the several checkpoints they had encountered along the way. The noncoms manning the checkpoints snapped to attention when they saw the officer escort and saluted him on through without delay.

Far out in the country, in a clearing by a splashing stream, the party had stopped while the driver broke out a packed lunch. At one point, Nawaz took a call on his satellite phone and stepped away from the others to talk privately.

Raj looked around at the tall trees, the rushing water. "This is the way Allah wants us to live," he observed. "Peace and quiet. In harmony with all things."

When Daniyal finished his portion of lamb and bread, he took out his well-thumbed copy of the al-Quran and sat by himself next to the stream, reading and meditating. After a while, the amir came over and settled down next to him.

"There is good news, Daniyal," Nawaz said. "We have dealt a blow on behalf of your family. It seems a police surveillance team has been watching your father's shop. One of those policemen has been eliminated on my orders. One of your friends from the madrassa has martyred himself in the process."

"Thank you for that, Amir. I am indebted to both of you. I do think of my family sometimes, what will happen to them."

"When it becomes known that the Reza family has given their son to religious purpose, the name will be honored by the righteous, by the millions. You will be the admired one because you will be the one closest to God." Nawaz turned and let his wandering eye play over the young man. "Before you were of the Reza family, Dani, you were first Allah's child."

After they had finished their lunch break, they completed the journey to the new safe house, a rambling old mansion that had been owned by an English lord in pre-Partition days. It was secluded and hidden from the highway by a long access road. The three young men were each assigned a spotless and comfortable room on the second floor. From their windows, they could see the surrounding hillside dotted with trees. There was not another house in sight.

After evening prayers, the young men who acted as servants provided a finely cooked beef-and-vegetable meal. The cold cucumber salad was wolfed down with delight. "Who would ever live in a place where they didn't have fresh cucumbers?" Nasir remarked.

It was well after nightfall when Nawaz called the three together. "Now we are ready for the next stage."

Several of the young servants came in with tape measures and notepads and started taking body measurements of the trio, like tailors attending to wealthy clients.

NINE

Pakistan was once called the most allied ally
of the United States. We are now the most nonallied.

ZULFIKAR ALI BHUTTO

After the shooting at the Anarkali bazaar, it did not take long for the police to come knocking once again on Awais Reza's front door. He'd been expecting it. This time the humane sergeant had been replaced by a straight-talking senior official.

"Where is your son Daniyal?" he demanded.

"I do not know."

"You told one of my men that you knew where he was but refused to say."

"That is not what I said. I said *if* I knew, I would not hand my own child over to the authorities."

"I ask you again, where is Daniyal?"

"I have answered this question. I do not know."

On a signal, several uniformed officers entered the house and commenced a search. Shez had been out shopping and came home to find strangers rummaging around in everything. She was ordered to sit with Awais for the duration of the search. She hated every second of the invasion of her home. Awais simply said, "Let them do their work, my dear."

"I don't think we have a choice."

The policeman showed Awais a photograph of a man lying on a morgue slab. "Do you recognize this man, Mr. Reza?"

Awais put on his reading glasses and took the picture. After a few moments, he handed it back and removed the glasses. "I don't think I've ever seen this man before."

"You are trying my patience, Reza. You must know this man. He was a close friend of your son's."

"I have met few of Dani's friends. This man in the picture I do not recognize."

"I find that hard to believe. You mean to say you do not keep an eye on your children and whom they are associating with?"

"They are grown men," Shez said politely. "Not children."

The policeman waved the corpse photo in Awais's face. "This friend of your son murdered one of my men in a cowardly ambush right in front of your shop at the bazaar. And you know very well that your shop has been under surveillance. I intend to find out everything I can about this Daniyal of yours."

Awais looked at him unblinkingly. Shez sat with hands clasped, head bowed.

The senior officer threw up his hands in disgust. "All right, that's enough. Let's continue our discussion down at headquarters."

∽

KAMRAN LEFT HIS DORM by a back door and took a roundabout walk across town to a farmers' market. He cast a wary eye behind him the entire way. He wore sunglasses, and his usual student-style shirt and tie had been exchanged for a plain, short-sleeved shirt. He cut through the market and headed into a half-filled parking lot behind an office building. Striding directly to a four-door Toyota, he climbed into the back. At the same time, the bodyguard got out of the car and stepped away, unfolding a newspaper.

In the backseat, Rania sat close to Kamran. "I don't know what you're going to say," she whispered, "but I don't care. I love you, and that won't change, no matter what. I meant what I said on the phone. I'm here, and you can't throw me away."

"I feel the same, Rania. We both know that. But we have to be prudent." He took in a breath and rushed out the words. "My father has been arrested."

Rania flinched. "*What*?"

"They think he knows where Dani is. The truth is, he hasn't the vaguest idea. But they don't believe him."

"But once they talk to him and see he's telling the truth . . . "

"These days, I don't trust the police to do much 'talking.' Rania, they'll probably beat him. Dani is on their radar screen, and they want him. They're probably wondering if the whole Reza family isn't somehow involved with the Taliban."

"But that's insane."

"And eventually they'll find that out. But by then our family's reputation will have been ruined. I'll probably be kicked out of school."

"God help us, no!" she erupted.

"Think about it, Rania. They're looking hard to arrest my brother, and they've already arrested my father. How long will it be before they come for me and Sallu? On the way over here, I was afraid I was being followed."

She picked up the bottle of spring water on the seat next to her and offered it to him. He shook his head.

"It comes down to this. For your own protection and that of your family, we can't let anyone know we're still seeing each other. I can't risk involving you in my problems. Not these kinds of problems."

Rania shook her head. "What kind of world are we living in?"

He laughed. "When I get a chance, I'll knock out a learned essay on that theme."

"I'll do whatever we have to do, Kami. You know that."

"I know."

"But just promise me this situation won't end it for us."

"It won't end it for me." He blew her a kiss. "Nothing will ever end it for me."

She drank some of the water. Her face was especially pretty in the shadowy sunlight. "So what are we to do now, my love?"

"I think the only thing we can do is make it look like we've cooled it, maybe even broken up. In fact, I'd prefer it to look like we've split up."

"No. I don't like that idea."

"Then let's make it seem like we're just not hanging out together as we were. There's no one at school who knows about our engagement plans."

"Well, that's not precisely true. I told a couple of the girls. But they won't say anything."

"We should just go to class as normal," Kamran said. "Only no more clandestine meetings every other day. We'd better keep it to once a week."

"Am I to speak with you during class?"

"Just do whatever is normal for the situation."

"Great," she said weakly.

"Don't forget, the police could be watching me. They could be tapping my cell phone, my computer too. We'd better not use e-mail. We can always exchange notes during class."

"Like little kids going behind the teacher's back."

"I'm sorry about all this, Rania." He ran his fingers through his hair, exasperated. "Suddenly I've got the police to worry about in addition to the hard-liners who say I've insulted their warped form of Islam."

They sat in silence for a few moments.

"I can imagine how your parents are going to react when they find out you were planning to marry a shady character."

"*Am* planning to marry a shady character," she corrected. "I know we're being tested. Our love is being tested. Allah has his ways."

"And mysterious ways they are."

"In the end, all of His ways are mysterious."

Kamran was silent and serious.

"We'll make it through this, Kami. We'll make it through. With Allah's help, we will make it through."

"The Reza family has been in Lahore since Pakistan was founded. My grandfather helped with resettlement after the British left. My father fought for Pakistan and almost lost his life in Bangladesh. We are honest people, loyal citizens of the nation we love. But now we are being looked at as enemies of the state."

"But it's all a mistake, and it will pass."

"I hope so."

Rania and Kamran parted somberly, each knowing that the test in front of them would strain their love to the breaking point. As Kamran walked away, the sedan pulled out of the parking lot and disappeared from sight. He cut back through the farmers' market and out onto the street, just another face in the crowd.

∞

WITH HIS FATHER in custody, Salman kept the shop open by himself for the whole day, just as Awais had done before he'd had a son to help out. With business the way it was, the effort was hardly worth it. He kept busy with inventory and bookkeeping. It was what his father would want.

In the late afternoon, the older man who owned the mobile-phone shop next door stopped in. Salman greeted him fondly: "Good to see you, Noor."

"Sallu, I am here to stand by you in these bad times. You know of my long friendship with your father. He is a good man and should not be blamed for the sins of another, even if it be his own son. His arrest is an outrage."

"They're really after Dani. But the thing is, Noor, we don't know what Dani is accused of. The police won't say."

"The authorities like to keep you in the dark as long as possible."

"It all has to do with that madrassa he's gone to the last few years," Salman explained. "They've arrested the whole staff. Suspected terrorists, they're saying. There was something in the paper about it, and I saw it on the Internet. One Google headline was saying the madrassa was a 'terror school.' Dani's imam was among those arrested."

Noor dropped his voice. "This I did not know. So maybe they only want to question Dani about the activities of this imam."

"That is our hope." Salman nodded toward the back room. "Shall we?"

Noor smiled. "Splendid idea. My son is watching the store."

Soon they were sitting in the cramped back room, passing the opium pipe back and forth. It did not take long to feel the warm relief seep through the soapy taste.

"This really does make life a little more bearable," Salman observed.

Noor held the smoke in his lungs until he was blue in the face, then gushed it out. "As Muhammad is the Last Messenger, I swear it is true. Opium in moderate partakings is a golden pleasure."

"I guess you heard about the shooting," Salman said.

"My son told me. You saw it?"

Salman nodded. "It was the policeman I told you about. The one who had been watching our shop."

"They were hoping Dani would show up here."

"He hasn't in a long time," Salman said. "Since he devoted himself exclusively to God, we have seen little of him. Here's the other thing, Noor. The man who shot the policeman was himself killed. I recognized him. He was a friend of Dani's. Dani brought him here to the shop once."

Noor slapped his hand to his forehead. "That would be suspicious to the authorities."

"I can't say I blame them."

"But Sallu, just because Dani knew the man, that doesn't mean he was involved in the shooting."

"That is what I told my mother."

"How is your dear mother?"

"Truly speaking, she's not doing well. I think it's the first time in years that my parents have been separated for even a night."

"Awais told me that when he was fighting in Bangladesh," Noor recalled, "your mother was informed that he had been killed, but she didn't believe it."

"That is so. She has more vision than most people. Extra sight. She did not believe it to be true. She *knew* he was alive and would come back."

"Allah answers all who ask with a pure heart," Noor said.

"But we must face our true situation," Salman said. "Look at us. Look at how we are forced to do immoral things in order to survive and keep our businesses going."

"It's always been that way, Sallu. And who can stop it? Just today I had to bribe a distributor in Karachi to get the right kind of batteries for these new-model smart phones. Without them, I'm out of business. They know that, Sallu, and they hold me up for twice the price."

"How much longer can we last like this? Every time there's a bombing, they go around and arrest a lot of people. Some are released; some we never hear from again. But does it stop these suicide attacks? In fact, they're happening with more frequency."

Noor shook his head in disgust. "At some point the military will come back and take power again, and we can forget about this democracy experiment. It doesn't seem to work here in Pakistan."

"If we let the Islamic parties take over," Salman said, "things will get much worse."

"Nobody I know wants their strict sharia law, but there are those who would like to see it happen."

"I blame the Americans for a lot of our troubles. Their wars are now our wars."

❧

SHEZ WAS DENIED admittance to the facility where Awais was being held. They cited some provision in a new law she'd never heard of.

"What does it mean?" she asked.

"It means, Mrs. Reza, you will not be able to see your husband."

"But when will he be released?"

"That is not our decision. It's up to the courts."

"What are the charges against my husband?"

"I do not have the authority to release that information. It's classified."

"Can you tell me if he's all right?" she pressed.

"I do not have that information."

Shez took the bus back home to Anarkali in a state of confusion, annoyance, and quiet desperation. Alone in the empty house, she reflexively began to clean things that didn't need cleaning. Later she made dinner for Salman and left it in the kitchen, then waited impatiently until the van came to take her to the hospital.

That evening on the nurses' floor, they knew all about the situation with Daniyal and Awais. As Shez checked in, she was called aside by the head nurse.

"The police were here to see me," she told Shez. "They asked a lot of questions about you and your family. I told them I knew little about your family and had only met a couple of them over the years. I told them I considered you one of my very best nurses. That you were dedicated to the sick and the injured." She put a comforting hand on Shez's shoulder. "I'm sure this is all some ridiculous mistake, and it'll all be sorted out. But for now, you have patients who need you."

It was a vote of confidence that Shez appreciated. Still, she was beginning to experience an emotion she had never really felt: shame.

∞

IN THE SECLUDED safe house outside Lahore, Daniyal, Raj, and Nasir were assembled in a room that Gul Nawaz had converted into an office. It was filled with the latest communications gear. The computer lines were routed through a black-box device used for encryption and firewalling.

"The foreigners are very clever with their surveillance technology," Nawaz was saying, "but we are more clever. They cannot detect this computer when it's on the Net. They cannot intercept any of our messages. Soon I will receive the signal I have been waiting for. We are about to take the glorious action we have been commanded!"

The three recruits sat up tall and straight.

Over the course of the next half hour, the amir explained some-thing of the spectacular event in which they would take part. It was to be a multiple-site attack. They would strike the infidels a crippling triple blow. "Now is the time for boldness, my friends. You must re-member that. Timing and positioning will be critical. You have each been selected for your devotion to the religious code, true, but also for your intelligence. It is important that we increase the number of fatalities beyond that of the shrine. Eliminating the infidel, that is our task. We must take away as many of these lost and damned souls from Allah's majestic presence as possible."

TEN

Why should I ask the wise men: Whence is my beginning?
I am busy with the thought: Where will be my end?

MUHAMMAD IQBAL

The city of Lahore had been suffering along with the rest of Pakistan, but after the bombing at the shrine, the ordinary range of deprivations was expanded and extended. The brazen attack on the holy site had, once again, made the government look clownishly inept against professional terror operatives. The media, especially in the West, was alleging involvement by Inter-Services Intelligence (ISI), Pakistan's intelligence agency. No one was fooled by Islamabad's all-out dragnet for suspects; it was seen as simply another attempt to refute negative perceptions of Pakistan's counterterror capabilities.

Nowhere was the crackdown more keenly felt than in the Reza family.

Awais Reza sat at a small table in a small room inside the main police building in Lahore. He looked tired, his beard scruffy and clothes wrinkled. Opposite him was a young lawyer, Zalman Khan, whom Shez had hired to help her husband, "stealing" the money from a stash Awais kept hidden in the false bottom of the mahogany wardrobe in their bedroom. After days of delay, the lawyer had been allowed to see his client.

"How is my wife?" was Awais's first question.

"She's safe, and she's okay but naturally upset. How are they treating you?"

"So far I've only been pushed around a little. But they're always threatening to get rough. Mostly they just do a lot of yelling."

"They've questioned you?" the lawyer prompted.

"About twice a day. They ask questions about my sons, my shop, whom I do business with, what mosque I go to. And I answer their questions. I tell them all I know. But they don't believe I know nothing of Dani's activities or where he could be hiding out."

Khan eyed him carefully. "You may speak in confidence with me, Mr. Reza. In fact, *do* you know where Dani is? You don't have to say where, just whether you know."

Awais shook his head. "Dani has been estranged from the rest of the family for a few years now. None of us really knows what he does, whom he does it with, or even where he is most of the time. We only know about the religious school and the hostel in Lahore, which the police know about."

"That is what your wife said."

"Why won't they let her visit me?"

"Mr. Reza, you are being held on a serious charge—aiding and abetting terrorist acts. The police are grabbing at anything to arrest those responsible for the shrine massacre."

"They suspect my son and also me?"

"They suspect everyone and anyone, including Mickey Mouse. However, I believe your case is like many that my colleagues and I have seen before. The authorities are casting a wide net and taking a lot of people into custody. But they have very little evidence against anyone. In your case, I do not believe the prosecutor has enough even to go before a judge, let alone lodge a trial request."

"I don't see what possible charges they would have against me."

"In the police report, they say you would not turn in Dani even if you did know where he is. Was that your statement to the investigating officer?"

Awais nodded. "These are the words of any father. Dani is my son, and no one has proven he's done anything at all. No, I would not turn him in if I knew where he was." He ran his fingers through his thinning hair. "For my sake and that of Shez, I wish I did know where he is and what he's doing. How long can they hold me?"

The young lawyer opened the flap of his leather briefcase. "I can show you the legal documents if you like. Under the new terrorism laws, they can hold suspects almost indefinitely. All they need is a certain level of suspicion."

"And what is my level of suspicion?"

"Because the charges are considered classified, we don't know if Dani is himself suspected of working with a terror cell in that madrassa he has been attending, but the imam they arrested was Dani's spiritual adviser. You see the problem?"

"So my son is under suspicion, and that means I am too."

Khan shook his head sympathetically. "I believe they intend to hold you, Mr. Reza, until Dani is found." He paused for emphasis. "And that could be a very long time indeed."

"Will they release me even if Dani turns up?"

"That is anyone's guess, Mr. Reza. It all depends on what they have on your son and what they might cook up against you. Look, it's standard in these cases for the prosecutors to use a threat against a family member to get a suspect to cooperate, to 'confess,' as it were. I believe this is what they are planning in your case."

Awais said, "So if Dani tells them what they want to know . . . they'll let me go. Is that what you're saying?"

The lawyer inclined his head. "Basically."

"And if Dani refuses to tell them anything?"

"It would go very badly for him, and it will not be so good for you."

Awais rubbed his face with both hands. "Things only get worse," he mumbled.

"Mr. Reza, your case will be thrown out at some point."

"I don't mean my situation gets worse. I mean our whole society. We're falling apart, and it gets worse every day. Our political system is hopeless. People go hungry while the elites get fat on imported luxuries. I don't mean to complain. I'm just another victim of the system, with all of its stupidity and greed."

"And its cruelty, I might add." Khan leaned closer and lowered his voice. "One final matter. I did not say anything to your wife about this, Mr. Reza, but there is an opportunity that I can take advantage of on your behalf if you wish. Our law firm is well known and highly respected. We have friends in the prosecutor's office."

The old soldier understood immediately. "And those friends can be accommodating."

Khan shrugged. "It's the system, Awais. I mention it only as a way to get you back with your wife and family as soon as possible."

"We all pay bribes to keep our shops open," Awais said resignedly. "Why shouldn't I pay to get myself out of this predicament?"

"It is strictly your decision. I can talk to Mrs. Reza about the money."

Awais thought for a few moments. "I don't know. We have hardly any savings left. Maybe I should wait and see if they just let me go."

"That is your decision. Can you deal with being in jail a while longer?"

Awais grunted contemptuously. "When I was in a POW camp after the Bangladesh war, we slept in an open compound under rain and sun. We rooted in garbage for food, and there were fights over a single aspirin. This place is like a luxury hotel compared with that. Yes, I'm a lot older now and don't wear as well, but I can handle staying put for a while. For now, don't tell Shez about your friends in the prosecutor's office. She'll insist on paying."

ﻬ

KAMRAN NEEDED A RIDE to Anarkali, and Zain offered to take him on the motor scooter. "Anything you need, Kami. Things are difficult these days. Friends have to help each other."

Kamran gave him a fraternal hug as he got on the back of the scooter. "Your friendship has always meant a lot to me, and now more than ever."

"You have more friends than you think, Kami."

Not far from the campus, they were stopped at a military checkpoint.

"I'll need some ID," the young soldier said. Kamran and Zain took out their student identification cards. "Shut off your engine." The soldier stepped away with the ID cards to confer with a ranking sergeant.

Zain killed the motor. "They're being pretty thorough."

"I don't like the vibes I'm getting."

The sergeant studied the two ID cards, then consulted a hand-held device for a few moments, pushing buttons and studying the screen. Finally he walked over to the scooter and looked from the picture on the card to Kamran. "Mr. Reza?"

"Yes, sir."

"You are a full-time student at the college?"

"Yes, sir."

The sergeant nodded and looked at Zain. "How about you?"

"Yes, we're both full-time students."

The sergeant walked around the scooter and looked it over. "This is your machine?"

"Yes, sir," Zain said. "It was a birthday present from my uncle."

More noncommittal nodding, as if that were the only response the man was authorized to give. "Mr. Reza, you are the brother of Daniyal Reza?"

"I am."

The sergeant was reading his handheld. "I see there is an alert out for your brother. Do you know his whereabouts?"

"No, sir. He doesn't stay in touch with our family."

The sergeant eyed him. "As Allah is your witness?"

"As Allah is my witness," Kamran pledged.

The sergeant glanced distractedly at the lengthening line of cars waiting to get through the checkpoint. He handed back the ID cards and moved away without a word. The young soldier came forward and motioned for them to continue on their way.

"That was nerve-racking," Kamran muttered as they drove off.

When they reached the Anarkali bazaar, there was a noticeable police presence, with uniformed men patrolling the narrow streets, which was not typical. They left the scooter in front of the shop and went inside.

Salman came out from the back and embraced Kamran.

"Sallu, you look overworked. I told you I can steal time away from school to help out here."

"No, no. You keep to your studies, little brother. I'm doing okay. Business is still down, so I've been closing early."

They all went into the small but comfortable back room, and Salman poured a round of cold tea from the cooler. "Zain, thanks for finding that lawyer, Khan. I spoke with him. He's good."

"One of the professors suggested him," Zain said. "I just got his phone number for Kami. He set it up."

"So what did the lawyer say?" Kamran asked.

"Abba won't do it."

"Oh, no."

"It's his decision, Kami. He thinks Mother doesn't know about the bribe. She's kind of angry he won't do it. The lawyer did say he looks to be in decent shape. Apparently he hasn't been tortured. Not yet anyway."

"He prefers to stay behind bars rather than buy his way out," Zain commented. "Maybe it's a matter of principle with your father."

Kamran said, "Yes, that's Abba, all right."

"He's always talked about honesty and a sense of pride," Salman added

"Has there been any word on Dani?"

"We've heard nothing," Salman said. "The lawyer says the police are looking for a lot of people, and Dani is just one of them."

"How long are they going to keep Abba locked up?"

"From what the lawyer told me, he won't get out till they find Dani."

Kamran shook his head sadly. "They're using him as a hostage to flush out Dani. I spoke with Ammi this morning. She puts on a good front, Sallu, but I know she is taking all of this very hard."

"She's rattled," his brother said. "She's doing extra hours at the hospital just to keep busy. What about you?"

"You mean, have the police come to see me yet?" Kamran said.

"No, but I'm expecting it any day." He told Salman about the stop at the checkpoint and being asked about Dani. "They're keeping watch on the Reza family."

"And what about you and Rania?"

"We're not seeing each other as much. It's not the right time. And a little too dangerous."

Salman looked pained. "I'm sorry about that, Kami. I know how much she means to you. Do they know at school about the police looking for your brother?"

"Some people know," Zain said. "Most don't. But word gets around fast on campus."

"If I'm arrested," Kamran said, "good-bye law school."

"On what grounds?" Zain asked. "You've got a great record. And besides, everybody knows you're totally against terrorism. Dani is, as they say, the black sheep of the family. Not you, Kami."

"And what about you?" Kamran asked his brother. "If they arrest me, they'll probably pick you up too."

Salman drank some tea and yawned. "I leave it in Allah's hands."

Kamran smiled. "I see you've been into the opium again."

"This I also leave in Allah's hands," Salman said, and they laughed.

∞

IT WAS AFTER evening prayers. The occupants in the safe house on the outskirts of Lahore were assembled in the room with the double doors and the large-screen TV. Daniyal, Raj, and Nasir were seated cross-legged on floor mats and had been served tea and sweet pastries by the respectful and silent young men. A slow-turning fan swept the room with a mild breeze. Gul Nawaz paced the carpet, his bushy beard combed and freshened, his rogue eye watchful and daring. As usual, his shirt was worn half unbuttoned to proudly show off the scar across his chest. What fighting the wound had come from no one ever said, nor did they have to. Clearly here was a shrewd and hardened warrior, a man one listened to.

"After our success against the sacrilege at the shrine, the people have even less respect for the government than they had a month ago. Allah's hand passes over the people's eyes, and they are opened. They see that they can no longer be protected by men who have not the wisdom of God to guide them. Men who pretend to adhere to the religious commands but then break the laws with alcohol and women, by cheating and stealing to enrich themselves. This is the enemy within our own land, disguised as our own countrymen, our own neighbors." Nawaz swung around to face the three sitting before him. "But we are not fooled! We know who are the devil's workers! We can smell them. They *reek* of Satan's foul presence. Now, observe this footage."

He turned to the big TV screen on the wall and used a remote control to call up some raw video footage of an open-air shopping plaza, surrounded by upscale shops, crowded and busy. The video played silently and had obviously been taken by a microcam hidden on someone walking through the plaza.

"Do we recognize this location?" the amir asked.

"That's the open shopping plaza downtown, the big one," Raj offered.

"Correct. A blasphemous place filled with decadent Western stores. Everywhere gaudy and lewd items on display for anyone to see, even our young women not yet of age. Many are seduced by these things into a life of degradation and sin." He pressed a button on the remote to freeze at the front window of a fashionable women's boutique. On display were mannequins in open-necked dresses, shorts, and skimpy tops. "This is the disgusting wear being offered to our women. And nothing to cover their heads! These are the clothes of a whore. The West hates Islam and the life we hold sacred. As they try to corrupt us, they deny the supremacy of Allah. They are trying to win over our women and girls with their music and their sexual dancing and these temptress getups."

The trio on the mats watched the screen with distaste as the footage switched to another part of the open-air plaza, where there was a sprawling food court with umbrella tables and fast-food vendors.

"Notice the people sitting around at these tables," Nawaz said. "Look at their ages. You see what we have here? The place is packed with young people, high schoolers and college kids. It's a meeting place for young men and women. They actually sit and talk together, eat together, even daring to touch. These are the children of the damned. These are the spawn of fornicators who dare to stand against all that is holy. And for what! Vulgar regalia and ugly music. They spit on our word and do the bidding of the infidels."

The amir stopped pacing.

"Between 3:00 and 5:00 of an afternoon, the food court is always crowded with these bastards of the false believers. One of you," he said, scanning their faces and pausing for effect, "one of you will strike here for the higher glory."

All three men erupted at once, each shouting for the honor of destroying the abomination so offensive to God.

Nawaz held up a hand. "Blessed are you who fight for rightful glory. But wait. This is only the first of three missions we will carry out on the appointed day." His grin was sharp-toothed and wolflike. "You see, we change tactics like the southern wind changes course. The shrine was one mission, carried out by two of our martyrs. This time we have three separate missions to accomplish, each carried out by a courageous believer. Again, observe closely."

Restlessness moved over the trio. The amir called up the next video footage. Again the camera was hidden on the body of a pedestrian. The image panned to reveal the exterior of a spacious office complex. "Here is one of the more infamous locations in Lahore. This is the headquarters of the regional police." He used the remote to speed up the footage, which flashed by until it froze on a street-level corner of the main building. "This is the office of the commanding officer and his staff, the people who oppress the righteous each day of the week. They ignore religious law and enforce the dictates of their masters in Washington. Every afternoon this area of the building is crowded with police officers changing shift." His lazy eye moved left and right. "One of you will have the honor of destroying these diseased parasites who prey on our people."

"Death to the oppressors," Daniyal responded.

A young man rushed into the room and whispered to Gul Nawaz. The amir listened for a few moments, then shouted a command. The three on the mats jumped to their feet.

"We have visitors," Nawaz said. "But they are not unexpected, so we are ready for them. Let us go quickly."

ELEVEN

We realize the importance of our voices
only when we are silenced.

MALALA YOUSAFZAI

Daniyal, Raj, and Nasir followed Gul Nawaz down a steep staircase into the candlelit basement. "It was thoughtful of the British to leave us this escape route," the amir quipped. At the bottom of the stairs, they were met by two men carrying flashlights and shoulder weapons. "*Go!*" Nawaz commanded.

Farther along, they came to an open door to what had once served as a coal bin. "All is ready," one of the men said and led them through the door into a dank passageway. Their rapid footfalls echoed off the crumbling concrete walls; Nawaz ignored his handheld radio, which was sputtering with an unreadable signal. They traveled fifty yards into the cavernous tunnel and then turned a corner. A little distance on, they reached an open metal hatchway encrusted with grass and earth. Nawaz barked an order, and the two flashlights went dark.

Within moments, all of them had scrambled through the small hatch and up a short ladder to emerge into a thick patch of trees. In the tinted moonlight, the old mansion loomed behind them, and from that direction the intermittent pop-pop-pop of gunfire could be heard. They hurried into the woods.

"Those are our men shooting," Nawaz said. "They were lying in wait."

They emerged from the trees into a small clearing. A black Humvee without lights was waiting. Emblazoned on the side was the crossed-saber logo of the army's special operations unit. A rear door was flung open, and a man in army fatigues jumped out. "Everything is ready, Amir!"

Without delay, Daniyal, Raj, and Nasir climbed into the back of the vehicle, followed by the man in fatigues. Nawaz got into the front passenger seat and muttered a few clipped words to the driver. The Humvee roared forward, crashing through tall weeds onto a rough path through the trees. The two men with shoulder weapons led the way on foot.

Gul Nawaz looked over his shoulder. "How many?"

"Only one squad," the man in fatigues replied. "I have deployed my men behind them. Behind them, Amir. The element of surprise is ours."

Nawaz pulled a light submachine gun from the rack on the dashboard. "Ha! They try to trap us. But it is they who are trapped!"

The man in fatigues was barking into his handheld radio. The three young men peered through the windshield as the vehicle barreled its way along the barely visible path, sideswiping trees and some brush, then back onto the trail.

"Look out!" Nasir shouted.

Three men in army uniforms leaped from behind trees and fired on the two runners. As they went down, Nawaz stuck the machine gun into the ballistic glass side port and shot off a long stream of rounds. The soldiers hit the ground. The driver swerved around the bodies of his fallen comrades, then jerked the wheel to run over the enemy soldiers. He threw on the headlights, and the night jumped back a hundred feet.

The Humvee ran free of the wooded tract and reached a paved road, where it pulled up short. The passengers could hear the muffled rattle of automatic weapons. Nawaz shouted a few code words into his radio. Instantly a reply crackled through. "Go!" he told the driver. "The way should be clear ahead."

The Humvee swung onto the road and rapidly picked up speed, passing a barren field with a small farmhouse off in the distance. As they rounded a curve, an armored car rolled out from the side of the road and opened fire. Rounds smashed into the windshield and bounced away. The driver whipped the steering wheel to his right. The Humvee ran onto the shoulder of the road and down into a ditch, where it came to a tilted stop. The tires spun uselessly in the grass.

Two soldiers came running across the road, firing rifles.

The man in the fatigues opened his door, leaned out, and discharged his machine pistol, dropping both soldiers. He swung out of the Humvee. "This way," he said. "Into the woods!"

∞

DESPITE HIS FAMILY and personal troubles, Kamran sat attentively in his constitutional law class, determined not to let those problems completely distract him from his education. He kept his eyes off Rania, sitting across the room, and she did not look his way.

"We have made agreements with the Americans," Professor Qasim was telling the class, moving around the floor. "We have accepted their money, lots of it. But we've paid a heavy price for that largesse. We have been drawn into their war in Afghanistan. In turn, this has brought terrorism to a new level here at home. Tens of thousands have been killed in various acts of violence. Almost daily, the foreigners employ flying missile launchers over our skies. Are the people really benefiting from the alliance with the West?"

This question was answered by shaking heads and a chorus in the negative.

"Of course the people are not benefiting," Qasim went on. "But then, who is?"

"The military," several students responded.

"Yes, indeed. The military is the main beneficiary of the billions this country receives from abroad. The generals take the majority of these funds for their own purposes. How that money is subsequently spent is hard to say. Reliable figures are impossible to obtain. But I point out that there are no costly troop deployments, no wars, no real reason that the military budget should be so high and kept so secret. We are not effectively combating the terrorist training facilities in the northern tribal belt, not using much manpower there. So where is the money going?"

"To Switzerland!" one student cracked.

"That we can assume," Professor Qasim said. "Now, consider this. Washington is fed up with the way our government and our military have been performing. And the people of Pakistan are also fed up. The Americans are demanding an end to official corruption. That is something the majority of Pakistanis have been striving for over the past three decades. The Americans are betting much on true democracy taking hold here in Pakistan. That is precisely what most educated Pakistanis would like to see. When viewed from these perspectives, it would appear that we have a few things in common with the United States. Any comments?"

"Yes, Professor," Kamran spoke up. "Both sides are hoping for democracy to work effectively here. However, the Americans need us as an ally in their terror war, no matter what kind of government is in power. They will quickly embrace another military dictatorship if it comes to that."

"Let's see hands," Professor Qasim said. "How many believe we are headed for another takeover by the military?"

Many hands shot up.

"How many think it will come soon?"

Once again hands went up all over the room.

After class, Kamran made his way to the main library. He had some research to do for an upcoming history test. He had to stay focused, no matter what frightful distractions surrounded him. While he was browsing alone among the back shelves, Rania appeared at his side.

"We can talk for a minute. There's no one around," she whispered. "How are you doing?"

"Okay. How about you?"

"Okay, I guess. Have you heard anything about your father?"

"The lawyer called my mother this morning. They're going ahead with formal charges, but Abba still refuses to pay a bribe to get out of it. At this point, I'm more worried about my mother than about my father."

"What do you mean?"

"It's all the pressure. She's worried sick over Abba, about Dani, about me and Sallu. Rania, I think she could be on the verge of a nervous breakdown."

"Your mother has been through a lot in her life. She's a strong woman."

"Up to a point, yes. I just hope she hasn't passed that point."

၁၀၁

A JAILER UNLOCKED the security door and admitted Awais to the interrogation room, where his lawyer, Zalman Khan, was waiting.

"How are they treating you?" Khan asked as they sat down at the counsel table.

Awais shrugged indifferently. "They keep me in my cell most of the time. The meals are thin and horrible. I'm losing weight, which is probably good. But I'm not being physically mistreated the way some in here are. At least they allow me to read newspapers. Who is this man coming to speak with me?"

"His name is Imran Abbas. He's an inspector with the regional counterterrorism task force. He is the one who signed off on the charges against you. I have the formal complaint with me. As I indicated last time we met, they are accusing you of complicity in terrorist activities."

"On what basis?"

The young lawyer leaned back in his chair. "Under the latest laws, you can be charged as a participant on the basis that you knew of a terrorist attack being planned and did not report it to the authorities. This is a violation by omission and can carry up to twenty-five years in prison."

Awais Reza sat calmly. Since early adulthood, he had faced catastrophe after catastrophe and had learned the importance of staying calm and thinking clearly. "For such a charge to stand up in court, they would have to prove I knew of some such terrorist plot. They won't be able to do that."

Khan opened his briefcase and pulled out a notepad. He riffled through several pages, then stopped to read his notes. "Do you know about the man who killed the policeman in the shooting near your shop in Anarkali? His name was Mohammad Kakazai."

"Yes, and I understand he was killed by the policeman. What about it?"

"The police have gathered statements placing Kakazai and your son Daniyal together at your shop. The way it is phrased in the indictment, they're making it seem like it was a strategy meeting for the bombing at the shrine, which Kakazai was involved in."

Awais flinched. "That is absurd. Yes, Dani once brought this man to my shop. He introduced him as a classmate at his madrassa. There was no 'meeting.' Dani needed some cash and was stopping by to pick it up. The other man was just tagging along. My son Sallu spoke with him for a few minutes. I did not. That's why I didn't recognize his picture when the police showed it to me. I barely noticed the man."

"Yes, I see in the report that you mentioned the cash to the police."

"Was that a mistake?"

The lawyer nodded. "Because you admit you gave money to Dani in the presence of this Pashtun gunman, they could make you look guilty as charged."

The door opened, and Inspector Abbas stepped into the room. He was a burly, officious bureaucrat, self-important and well fed. "Are we ready, Counselor?"

"Given the skimpy information I've been provided," Khan said, "I'd say we're as ready as we can be, Inspector."

"*Thank* you," Abbas said without much courtesy. He took a seat, laid a file folder on the table, and plunged in. "Mr. Reza, have you been advised by your attorney of the charges we have filed against you?"

Awais nodded.

"And do you understand that should you be convicted of any of the charges, you face considerable time in prison?"

"Yes."

"For a man of your age, such a sentence would be for life." When Awais remained unmoved, the inspector blurted out, "You're sure to die in a prison cell."

The lawyer leaned forward. "It remains to be seen, Inspector, if Mr. Reza will ever be convicted of anything."

For a few moments, the bureaucrat busied himself with the papers in the file folder. "Back in February, Mr. Reza, you received a known terrorist at your shop, Mohammad Kakazai by name. He was accompanied by your son Daniyal, who attended the same madrassa as this terrorist. You have confessed to this. You have also said you gave money to them. Isn't that your statement?"

"My son needed some cash for living expenses," Awais stated flatly. "I gave a small sum to him. It was not meant for this man Kakazai or the madrassa."

"Yes, that is your statement. Not very long after you gave Daniyal the money, the plot to blow up the shrine was set in motion. This was at the same madrassa where Kakazai and your son were being schooled in extremist thought. The jury is going to find your actions highly suspicious, Mr. Reza, since Kakazai is known to have been involved in setting up the attack on the shrine. However, in the interests of expediting your case, I am prepared to show a certain amount of leniency. In exchange for your guilty plea to reduced charges, the prosecutor will ask for no more than a five-year sentence."

"Five years in prison? For what? I am innocent of these ridiculous charges."

The inspector looked at the lawyer. "Does he understand that we have incriminating evidence?"

"Let's be frank, Inspector. My client is innocent. Your 'deal' is built upon flimsy, circumstantial, and misrepresented evidence. In a courtroom, if you will permit me, sir, I will shoot holes in your case."

The inspector turned to Awais. "Are you willing to gamble your life on the possibility that you'll be acquitted?"

Awais Reza was less heated than the other two. He sat erect, motionless, not wasting any energy. "I have Allah as my witness—I have done nothing unlawful. Why should I give away five years of my life just so you can win a case? Yes, Inspector, I will gamble that an impartial trial will clear my name and justice will prevail."

Now the inspector was impatient. "Mr. Reza, your own son has been part of a terror cell operating out of his madrassa in Lahore. Your own son is friends with a known terrorist, a man who helped engineer the attack. Your son brought this terrorist to your shop. Money was handed over at that time. Mr. Reza, don't be fooled. You stand a very real chance of being convicted of complicity and sent to prison for the rest of your life. I am offering you a way out, a chance to eventually be reunited with your family."

Awais shook his head. "It is more important that I not disgrace my family than that I be with them. I will not confess to sins I have not committed."

With a grunt of contempt, Inspector Abbas took up his file folder and walked out.

"Now what?" Awais asked.

The lawyer looked at his hands. "I have an idea. You won't like it, but it will keep you from going to trial. Let's face it; we could lose at trial. I don't think we would, but you never know how a jury is going to interpret the evidence."

"What is this idea I won't like?" Awais asked.

"The prosecutor knows he has a weak case, but he knows there is a strong antiterror mood in the country right now. It might tip the balance in his favor. My idea is to go for a sentence of no more than a year in jail. Remember, Mr. Reza, you could be waiting in here a year before any trail gets under way. I could probably get the charges knocked down from complicity to simple unlawful association. Please think about it."

∞

After abandoning the disabled Humvee, Gul Nawaz and his men fled from the pursuing soldiers into the dark and heavily wooded terrain beyond the farms and empty fields. Nawaz tried radioing his backup team but could not raise them. Instead he decided to prepare a trap—an unexpected ambush. The amir had everyone take cover and wait. When a group of pursuing soldiers was close enough, Nawaz's machine gun opened up while the man in the fatigues emptied the magazine of his machine pistol. With four more of their men down, the rest of the soldiers gave up the chase and retreated back into the night.

Daniyal, Raj, Nasir, and the Humvee driver ran ahead through the moonlit forest while the two men with weapons followed them as a rear guard. There was no real trail, just endless trees and tall weeds. After a while, they heard a helicopter approaching.

"They have night vision!" Nawaz barked. "Everyone get behind a tree! Keep it between you and the bird."

The chopper came in low over the trees, then swept around, making pass after pass. Nawaz kept his face to the sky, watching, waiting. Soon the helicopter moved slowly overhead and began to hover. Nawaz lifted his machine gun and took aim.

Abruptly a bright beam speared down from the noisy craft, daylighting a patch of woods.

"Do not move!" the amir yelled.

The light started to spread.

Nawaz pulled the trigger, spewing bullets.

The light beam flashed out in a spray of debris. The helicopter wobbled from side to side, tipped over, and headed down. As it sank into the treetops, the rotor blades tore away, spinning off. The fuselage hit the ground with a screech of twisting metal, followed by a thud as the gas tank exploded. Burning debris rained down among the trees.

Nawaz and the others quickly left the wreckage behind them. A couple of miles on, they came to a rocky stream. "We rest here, but only a few minutes," Nawaz said.

The three young men sat on the bank of the stream and splashed water on themselves. The night was warm; they had been running off and on for miles. The amir tried his main lieutenants on the radio but was still unable to raise anyone, even on the hailing frequency. He tried his cell phone but could not get a signal.

The group huddled together by the cool stream, and the Humvee driver spoke up. He'd lived in the area for years and knew of a farm not far away where they could probably find some kind of vehicle, along with plenty of petrol. He had worked on the farm as a teenager and knew it well. The amir considered this, then called for silence and began to pray, asking for guidance. After the proper words were said and the prayer was over, Nawaz agreed to the driver's plan. "Lead the way."

They crossed the shallow stream and hiked into another stand of woodland. An hour later, they reached their destination. It was not a large farm, but there was a substantial house, outbuildings, and fields with sprouting crops. They made their way to the main barn. Inside, there were several farm machines—among them a sturdy pickup truck.

TWELVE

But I knew that what had happened was an eye-opener
not only to the United States but also to Pakistan,
who realized that after what has happened on
the 11th of September, it was simply impossible
to continue to play those games in Afghanistan.

LAKHDAR BRAHIMI

As it had been all week, foot traffic at the Anarkali bazaar was way down, so Salman closed up shop early at 10:00. His friend Noor from the mobile-phone store also decided to call it a night, and they walked home together.

"You can't blame the customers for staying away," Salman said. "Most of the time, the whole city is without power. And now we've got all these damn police checkpoints to deal with. You take your life in your hands just going shopping."

"It's smarter to stay home. Business suffers, but what's new?"

"Have you noticed? The food lines are getting longer."

"We're in for another round of shortages," Noor said. "I see wheat prices are going up again."

On this occasion, their journey home was unhindered. There were no roving security stops along the way. Salman and Noor shared a warm hug and praise to Allah upon parting. In such times, it was unknown when they might next see each other. When the government couldn't be relied upon, or even trusted, personal safety and well-being became a daily uncertainty.

"I hope you're hungry," Shez called out from the kitchen as Salman entered the candlelit house. Four nights a week now, she was on duty at the hospital, but on her evenings off, Shez waited up and had dinner ready when Salman returned from the bazaar. It was her way of maintaining a sense of normalcy when there was none.

"Business is still bad," Salman said as he ate his reheated vegetable stew. "But I think I can cover expenses this month. Did you talk to the lawyer?"

Shez put down her spoon; it had been days since she'd had any kind of appetite. "He called me. They're going ahead with a trial. Which might not be for a year or more. Without a bond, Awais will have to remain in jail until then."

They sat in silence for a while; it was the silence of dwindling hope.

Finally Salman said, "We've *got* to convince him to pay that bribe."

"The lawyer has urged him several times to pay, but your father still refuses." She reached out and touched her son's hand. "That is his wish, and I respect that. But his wish is not my wish. As Allah means it to be, I will not allow my husband to be caged like an animal. Not if I can help it . . . I've decided I'm going to give the lawyer the money, without telling Awais."

"I think that is best, Ammi. I really do."

"I don't know what's best, Sallu. I just want him back home. The lawyer says once the money is paid, Awais will be given a small bond and released."

"Will they drop the charges against him?"

"No, that would require a separate and larger payment. We don't have it right now, but we have to get him out first. By the time the trial is scheduled to start, we will have saved enough to get the charges dismissed. It's the only way out of this nightmare that I can see."

Salman nodded thoughtfully. "Yes, with a little time we could raise the extra money. I even have some jewelry I could sell. Whatever we have to do, Abba belongs here at home."

Later, Salman settled into his small bedroom and looked over the Lahore newspaper by candlelight. He had never married but eight years earlier had been engaged to a girl from a good local family. When she had been killed in an auto accident in downtown Lahore, Salman had been so distraught that he had thought no more of marriage. "Maybe someday, but not now," he told his parents.

Shez came to the doorway to bid him good-night. "I remember when you and Dani were little," she said, more to herself than to her son, "before Kami was born. You two were always together. You were the big brother, and Dani was the little one who looked up to you." Suddenly she was near tears. "How did we lose him? How did we lose him?"

Salman put the newspaper aside. "It was nothing you and Abba did," he assured her. "It's really nobody's fault. It's just that some people develop extreme feelings about religion. Who can say why?"

"I blame those radicals at the madrassa," Shez said. "Brainwashing these young men into doing their dreadful bidding."

"That's it exactly. These extremist leaders have hijacked Islam and twisted it around to serve their own ends. If they did snare Dani with their lies and distortions, that's not the fault of our family, Ammi."

Shez dabbed at her eyes with a tissue. "To lose a child . . . " she started, then turned away. "Good-night, son."

∽∞∾

AT THAT MOMENT, while his mother was confused and broken-hearted in Anarkali, Daniyal was far outside Lahore, sitting with his comrades at a fine table, enjoying a meal of fresh fish and roasted vegetables.

Gul Nawaz had again proved his far-reaching resourcefulness. Once they had stolen the pickup truck and driven north on country roads for some miles, Nawaz had finally got a mobile signal that would hold. He had made several calls, talking loudly and very fast, mostly in coded set phrases. Within an hour, he had been directed to yet another of the network's safe houses. This one was something of a modern palace, with many rooms on three stories, situated on a large, walled-off estate. It was owned, Nawaz took pride in explaining, by an elite member of the local government who held a secret passion for Islamic supremacy. He had helped fund the attack on the shrine. "Allah's servants come from many walks of life," the amir reminded his acolytes.

After the sumptuous meal, fresh clothes and footwear were provided for all by the household staff, who treated their unexpected guests with shy deference and a certain amount of trepidation. They strictly avoided looking directly at Gul Nawaz's bad eye.

Once they had refreshed themselves and spent time in prayers of thanksgiving, Daniyal, Raj, and Nasir were called into the plush home theater for a status report.

"The engagement with the infidels has once again proven our strength," Nawaz said. "I have learned that we killed more of them than they killed of our people. Praises!"

"Bless our fallen comrades!" Nasir exclaimed.

"I can tell you that word has already reached our friends in the north. They compliment us on the downing of the helicopter. It is a further embarrassment for the government. Each and every day, we show the people how weak and ineffective their godless leaders are."

"This is a divine plan," Daniyal spoke up.

"It is, to be sure," Nawaz agreed. "Now, let us turn to our main concern—jihad. Our threefold mission to destroy the comfort and sanctity of the infidels has not changed in the slightest. We are merely delayed a short time."

∽

KAMRAN AND ZAIN were having lunch in the crowded cafeteria at the Student Center. They had chosen the daily special, which wasn't very special.

"Sometimes I feel kind of useless," Zain was saying, "sitting in classes all day discussing all these fancy ideas about politics and the future of Pakistan—will democracy ever work here, and how can we elect people who aren't corrupt, and all that. . . . Meanwhile, against all the talk going on in the universities, we've got a population out there that's half starved most of the time. What good does all of our talk do the average citizen?"

Kamran nodded. "Put that way, talk can never do any good. Which you know is not true. But I know what you mean. We sit around debating like philosophers while the people go hungry." He leaned over his iced tea. "But that's what this is all about, my friend. Our effort to become lawyers. It's the only way we can help Pakistan get on its feet. To a certain extent, lawyers run this country."

"You're always talking about human nature. Do you think it's part of human nature to steal and cheat, enriching yourself at the expense of others?"

"To a certain degree, yes," Kamran said. "It's probably some instinct, some evolutionary process—secure your own existence first and foremost. Selfishness is part of human nature. Call it a survival mechanism. Just as I'm sure there's even some evolutionary programming at work when it comes to man's perpetual impulse for war. Maybe that's the way we had to live for unknown thousands of years in order to survive as a species." Kamran grinned. "That biology course taught me a few things about the human animal."

Zain nodded. "The art of civilization comes down to overcoming our own natural instincts and prejudices. Then that means our government, our leaders, our political and military elites aren't very civilized. Talk about your 'human animal'!"

"Well put."

They finished eating and went their separate ways. "Be safe," they said to each other, as they always did when parting.

Kamran took the steps down to the concourse, where hundreds of students were milling around or heading off to class. As he cut over to the main building, an older man in a fine linen suit emerged from the crowd and made eye contact with him.

"Mr. Reza," he said, "may I have a couple of minutes of your time?"

Kamran sagged. So this was how the police came for you, polite and harmless—then they put the cuffs on you. For a moment, he couldn't speak.

"Please do not be alarmed, Kami," the man said and extended his hand. "I'm Jamal Omar, Rania's father."

Kamran broke into a grin and shook hands. "How do you do, Dr. Omar? Rania has spoken of you many times."

"Not all of it complimentary, I assume," Dr. Omar said.

"On the contrary, sir. She speaks highly of her parents. She told me about your job at the hydroengineering department for the Punjab. Very interesting work, sir."

"It can be," Dr. Omar said, looking toward some stone benches by a small reflecting pool. The lunch hour was nearly over, and the area had begun to empty out as students headed back to class. "Can we sit for a moment?"

The older man spoke fluently and unself-consciously. He had a clean-shaven, weathered face. It was an honest face, that of a man with a clear conscience. "Rania has confided in me about your relationship," Dr. Omar began. "She has told me about you, Kami, about winning a scholarship to get into college. I understand your grades are among the highest in your class."

Kamran shrugged modestly. "It was nice of Rania to mention that."

"She has been a little more forthcoming with me than she has with her mother. I know you two are pretending to be estranged, acting as if you are not keeping company any longer. Rania says it's just for the time being."

Kamran could feel the sweat coming out on his forehead. "That's true, sir."

"As I understand it, if I may be blunt, Kami, your brother is being sought by the police. He's supposedly mixed up in this bombing or some such terrorist business."

Kamran was studying his hands. "We're not sure exactly what he's accused of, Doctor."

The man looked off into the distance, lining up his words. "Now, I understand they have taken your father into custody."

"Yes, sir."

"He is also accused of terrorist activities?"

For a moment, Kamran sat in silent shame. "Yes, but his lawyer says they're just charging him so he will tell them about my brother Dani." He looked directly at Dr. Omar. "Abba has no idea where Dani is or what he's doing. The police don't believe him."

Omar was nodding, understanding. "That is a favorite game of theirs, playing one person off another."

"We're not a terrorist family, sir, if that's what you came to ask me about."

The older man smiled. "Oh, I know that, Kami. Rania has told me enough about your family for me to understand the situation."

"Thank you."

"It seems your brother has fallen for the same foolishness a lot of young and disillusioned people fall for. Radical change. Islam is the way, and all that stuff. But I know that your father runs a respectable shop in the Anarkali bazaar and that your other brother works alongside him. Your mother is a nurse. And you, you're a fine, upstanding college man with a future. No, you're not a terrorist family, that's for sure."

Kamran wiped his hand over his brow. "I appreciate your realizing that, sir. But you have something else on your mind, I believe."

"Kami, my daughter's welfare is a major concern. These are dangerous times. Many people are vanishing into official custody. Unfortunately, your situation is very troublesome to me, you and Rania meeting on the sly now and then. Even with a bodyguard to watch out for her, I am constantly worried. I'm going to ask you to forgo even those occasional meetings, Kami, at least until we see what happens with your father and your brother. Does that sound unfair?"

Kamran looked down. "No, it's the right thing to do, sir."

Dr. Omar put his hand on Kamran's shoulder. "Thank you for understanding."

∞

AWAIS WAS CALLED early out of his tiny single cell and taken to the interrogation room, with its rough-worn counsel table and wooden chairs. As before, the lawyer Zalman Khan was waiting. "Sit, sit, Mr. Reza. You look tired."

"Who can sleep when there's all this yelling and talking at night? They keep the corridor lights on so they're always in your eyes." He had finally been allowed to exchange his own wrinkled and dirty clothes for a baggy but clean prison outfit. He fixed the lawyer with an unflinching gaze. "You have news?"

"I've had a chat with the prosecutor." Khan stood up from the table, put his hands in his pants pockets, and looked around as if there were something to see. "First off, my boss had an informal conversation with the prosecutor's boss, a phone call. They both went to Oxford. The so-called old-boy network still extends from London to Islamabad. A lot of the elites in this country are more English than Pakistani. Anyway, my boss got the prosecutor to admit—quite off the record, understand—what we already had surmised, that they were leaning on you for leverage against Dani. In other words, they're not really looking to hook you into this nasty business. But they have to look like they're pulling out all the stops to fight the Taliban and these other terrorists."

Awais nodded. "I know what you mean."

"I visited the prosecutor at his home last night," the lawyer went on. "I told him what my boss had said, that you were just a pawn in this case and aren't really the object of their investigation." Khan walked the floor a moment. "He was honest and straightforward with me. He said your case is an example of their new policy of 'extended reach,' as he called it. Orders from Islamabad. The government simply must look tough on terrorism. He did not deny it when I told him it was all about pressure from Washington. Oh, yes, Mr. Reza, international politics comes into your case. On that level, the prosecutor tells me, his hands are more tied than normal."

"He's still asking for a five-year sentence?" Awais asked.

"That was his story at the beginning of our talk. Fortunately, the prosecutor is not a very devout Muslim, and he broke out a bottle of French wine." He grinned. "In the interests of your case, I was forced to share a glass with him. Or was it two? The point is, the wine got him to loosen up a little. So I pleaded your case. You are innocent of all the charges, a victim of a state trying to impress foreign interests that it is working hard to stamp out terrorist groups. He conceded that I was viewing the situation clearly. I asked that you be given a one-year sentence at most. He came back with an offer of two years. It's just so he can show he's doing his job. Two years, Mr. Reza, and they'd probably let you out early. You might only do a year and a half."

Awais reacted by stroking his beard, now longer than he liked to keep it. "But I would have to plead guilty to horrendous things. This would bring shame and dishonor on my family."

The lawyer sat down at the table. "If we turn down the offer and go to trial, even if you are found not guilty, there will always be those who will think you got away with something."

"I realize that," Awais said. "But an admission out of my own mouth is a different thing, Mr. Khan. It carries all the disgrace of the traitor."

The lawyer nodded his understanding. "So even if I got the sentence cut down to a year, six months, whatever, you'd still say no to a guilty plea."

"I don't do it lightly. I've thought this over many times. I would never be able to live down the shame of having admitted to helping the extremists. These are people I despise and, yes, even hate. It is enough that I have lost my own flesh and blood to these animals with their sick distortions of Islam. To add to this awful legacy by saying I was myself involved would be more than I can take." He threw up his hands in disgust. "Better I should just go to prison for whatever length of time and be done with it."

"You realize, Mr. Reza, that if we go to trial and the jury comes back with a guilty verdict, that could mean twenty years in prison."

"No, it wouldn't," Awais asserted. "I'd be dead long before my sentence was up."

THIRTEEN

Who has suffered? The families of the dead, no doubt.
But a greater loss was inflicted on Pakistan because,
as I said, we lost the pillars of our society.

PERVEZ MUSHARRAF

The palatial safe house outside Lahore that had been put at Gul Nawaz's disposal was proving to be a perfect staging base for his displaced fighters. It was large, well hidden, comfortable, and stocked with supplies. With a laptop computer belonging to the home's absent owner, Nawaz logged on to his encrypted "cloud computing" account and picked up right where he'd left off before the disruption and relocation. Orders were securely sent, messages safely received. According to Nawaz, foreign intelligence put out a lot of disinformation about its ability to intercept online transmissions. However, it was known that it was not able to crack a whole range of encryption methods, and it was these that were used by the extremist networks to freely communicate.

During the day, vehicles came and went. Some of Nawaz's aides met with him in private. Some stayed; others left with their orders. It was business as usual. The operation was getting under way.

The three bombers spent time across the courtyard in the private mosque. Theirs were prayers of devotion and joy, hatred and conviction. Of the three young men, Daniyal was proving the most intensely devout. "You have the rapture of God upon you," Raj said.

"I saw this from the first time we met," Nasir added.

Daniyal accepted their remarks with humble pride. "I am honored to be with my brothers."

There was a full workout gym in the basement, and the three young men took advantage of it during their enforced idleness. They spent hours on the treadmills and weight-lifting benches. Afterward there were hot showers and a steam room to reinvigorate tired muscles. The luxurious villa also included an indoor shooting range. The owner kept a small arsenal of pistols and rifles on hand, with cases of ammunition. The three young men practiced target shooting, making a game of it, not taking it seriously. Firearms would not be their instruments of divine retribution.

After evening prayer and another fine meal prepared by the able staff, the three young men wandered into the TV room. For a while, they watched a cartoon and even laughed here and there at the characters' silly antics. When the show was over, they switched to the Geo News channel, as they had been doing regularly. Coverage of the government's security crackdown was always the top story. This time there was a report on the downing of the army helicopter in pursuit of members of a Taliban splinter group. When footage of the wreckage came on the screen, the three men cheered and brandished their fists in the air.

"During the courageous pursuit of these desperate men," the reporter was saying, "many were killed, while the army reports the loss of only two soldiers."

That brought a loud jeer: "Lies!"

Now the footage cut to close-ups of the wanted terrorists. The reporter called off names, and pictures were flashed on the screen. When Daniyal saw himself in a snapshot taken the previous summer at school, he threw his hands upward. "I take this as a blessing, as a further sign of His approval."

"Can you imagine the news reports after we have carried out our mission?" Raj said.

Nasir jumped to his feet. "The very skies will fall upon them!"

இ

AT THE ANARKALI BAZAAR, Salman got to the store later than usual. Everyone had already put up their canvas awnings to shade the storefronts against the intense summer sun. When all the merchants did the same, the awnings created cool lanes for shoppers to stroll along. Salman spent ten minutes erecting his own awning, although with the slowdown in business, it hardly seemed worth the time.

Salman went into the back of the store and took out a thick envelope from inside his shirt. Reaching up to a crowded shelf, he found a bubble-pack mailer. He placed the envelope inside and sealed the pack shut. He did not fill out the address label.

While he was hiding the package on a shelf, the bell over the front door sounded. A middle-aged man and his wife came in, and Salman went out to greet them with his best shopkeeper manners. "May it please you that I can be of service."

"You must be Awais's son," the man said.

"Yes, I am Salman."

"I'm used to dealing with your father when I buy any kind of jewelry."

Salman smiled. "Yes, but please understand, I have been trained by my father, as he was trained by his father. Our family is known here in the bazaar for quality merchandise and fair prices. We've been here for three generations now."

"Yes, the Reza name is respected even by your competitors. But I would prefer to see Awais. When will he be in?"

Salman bit his lip. "I'm afraid . . . Abba is out of town, visiting relatives. I will be happy to assist you in anything you have in mind. You mentioned jewelry."

"When will he be back?"

"Not for a couple of weeks, sir. If you'd care to wait until then . . . "

The wife took over and hushed her husband. "No, we can't wait that long, young man. I'm looking for something special, a graduation gift for our daughter."

Salman went into his salesman's routine. He had a naturally plausible and easygoing way that played well with female customers. "The power of the purse is with the ladies"—he had never forgotten his father's advice. He showed the wife to the jewelry counter and produced several stunning items for her to consider: a bracelet in silver, a large pin with a diamond center, a necklace with an immaculate pearl section. These were each looked at but passed back. The lady was almost tempted by a set of earrings in jade and platinum. Still, she could not be persuaded to buy. Finally Salman showed her an elegant little tiara of sterling silver, with pavé diamonds in the front. Instantly she fell in love with it.

"She *is* a princess, and this will be perfect! Look, dear. Isn't this just perfect for our darling princess Lyla?"

The husband was busy at another glass case, studying the selection of wristwatches, and hardly glanced at his wife. "Yes, very nice."

She winked at Salman. "He doesn't know jewelry from cricket bats. We'll take the tiara. Can you gift-wrap it for me?"

"Certainly, ma'am. A very smart choice. I'm certain this will be a lifetime keepsake for your daughter."

Salman had all he could do to keep his composure as he headed into the back room to wrap the tiara in its lovely velvet gift box. The little tiara was among the most expensive items in the shop. This would be the best sale they'd had in months! And the customer hadn't even bothered asking the price.

When he brought out the wrapped package, the lady was all smiles and gratitude. She had a wad of rupee notes in her hand.

"Young man," the husband called out, "this watch here in the case. May I see it?"

Salman adopted a nonchalant manner as he brought out the silver watch. "I see it is not only your wife who has fine taste, sir. This is one of the world's great wristwatches. Automatic self-winding. Of course, those are diamonds around the bezel. It has a few interesting complications—such as the moon-phase calendar, the dual stopwatch, and the multi-time-zone function."

The man slipped the heavy watch onto his wrist to admire its bold, masculine look and feel. He held up his arm for his wife's approval. "Well . . . what do you think?"

"Something tells me it doesn't matter what I think, dear. If you like it, that's enough for me."

"You hear that, Salman? I have permission to spend a little of my own money. Very well. You've just made another sale. Your father will be proud of you."

Salman lapsed into an almost pious tone. "Allah favors me with the very wisest of customers," he professed. "Customers with sophisticated tastes and fine judgment. I am honored that you have allowed me to serve you in my father's absence."

They paid cash with fresh banknotes, and Salman locked the money away in the safe. He celebrated the two remarkable sales with a few puffs on the opium pipe. While he was enjoying himself, a bicycle messenger arrived and announced, "Package for pickup!"

Salman retrieved the padded envelope he had hidden and handed it to the messenger. "I assume this will get to its destination shortly."

"I'm headed back to the office now," the messenger said, already out the door.

Salman went back to the opium pipe and began to think. Then he took out a tiny calculator and began entering figures. He got up and consulted a price list, then did some more figuring on the calculator. There was a look of confusion on his face. When he put the calculator away, Salman lowered his head in silent prayer.

He called his mother on the cell phone. "Remember what you said this morning? That Allah would watch out for our family?"

"Of course," Shez said. "This I believe with all my heart."

"Well, it has come true, Ammi. I just sent off the money to the lawyer's office, as you instructed."

"So that is done. We will have Awais home soon."

"But Ammi, listen. Allah sent me two customers who bought some of the most costly merchandise we have for sale. Ammi, I just did the figuring on the sale, what our costs were and what profit we made. Guess what? The profits equal what we are paying to get Abba free. Even a little extra."

"It is a sign, Sallu," she murmured. "Allah is on our side."

∽∾

KAMRAN WAS PARTLY resentful that he had allowed himself to be persuaded by Rania's father to cut all ties. "For the time being," Dr. Omar had said. Yet those stolen moments with Rania had been an oasis in a desert of despair. Still, in a way, it was a relief not to have contact right now. Ever since he'd been roughed up and threatened for openly escorting her, he had been worried that something would happen to her simply because she was associated with him. The Islamic hard-liners at school were a disgrace to the religion, but they were capable of violence and might act on their morbid impulses. Rania could easily become a focus of their wrath. It had made him physically sick when he had read about a teenager who had had her nose sliced off because she had briefly danced in public with a boy. What if something like that happened to Rania? It would be his fault.

And right now, it was all much worse. His family had fallen under the intense suspicion of the authorities. For most decent people, there was dishonor in just being suspected of a crime. Dr. Omar had been right. His daughter should stay as far away from Kamran as possible.

"But it's only till this situation clears up," Zain was saying consolingly.

Kamran was in his dorm room, eased back in his desk chair, arms folded. "I hope that's true. For Rania's father to take time out of his busy day to come and see me . . . it kind of hit home how serious things have gotten."

"Have you spoken with Rania?"

"No. Her father wants to tell her about us not seeing each other. That's best. I've got a class with her this afternoon. It's going to be tough."

"You still want to go over to Anarkali tonight?"

"I should," Kamran said. "My mother is under a lot of strain, and so is my brother."

Zain was headed out the door. "Let's leave about seven. I'll be out in front on the scooter. Be well."

As soon as his classmate left, Kamran turned back to his laptop and the online lecture he needed to get through for a lesson on wills

and trusts, an important subject but tedious and filled with legal mi-
nutia and ancient terms. It was his habit to concentrate fully on his
studies, putting all else out of his mind. But the situation with Rania
kept coming back to him. How would she react? Would she be angry
because he'd given in to her father's wishes? That would be like her.
He had to keep in mind what she had told him: Allah was testing
their love. It was a test he could not afford to fail. Even this short separation was heartbreaking.

Half an hour later, Kamran finished the online lecture. He saved
his notes to a flash drive and logged off the computer. One more
chore and he'd be caught up on homework. He hunched over the
desk and opened a textbook on forensic chemistry.

Zain rushed into the room without knocking and closed the
door. "I was in the senior lounge just now, watching the news. They're
showing pictures and naming suspects in the bombing. One of those
pictures was of Dani."

Kamran lowered his head limply, like a wounded bird.

"Danish Hassan was watching with me. He'll blab it all over
school. I know you guys don't like each other."

"You know what, Zain? I'd like to cut class and go see my mother
now."

"I understand."

"She's going to freak out. I don't want her to see Dani on the
news. I'd rather she heard it from me first."

A few minutes later, the two of them left the dorm by the back
fire stairs and reached the student parking lot, where Zain had a re-
served space for his motor scooter. They hopped on the bike, Zain
gunned the engine, and they rolled out along the driveway. Before
they passed the main building, the head secretary from the dean's
office came out of a side door and flagged them down. Zain pulled
over to the curb. "Yes, Mrs. Rahat?"

"Kami, you're wanted in the admin building. Dr. Tasman's office."

"Does it have to be now, ma'am?" he asked. "I have something important to do."

"This is pretty important."

Zain drove him around to the front of the campus. "Good luck," he said as Kamran dismounted and hurried away. "I'll wait for you, Kam."

Nervously, Kamran hiked across the plaza to the administration building. He took the elevator to Dr. Tasman's fourth-floor office. Tasman was sitting behind his desk; as always, he was attired in a three-piece banker's suit perfectly tailored for his stout, middle-aged frame.

"Please sit down, Kamran."

Kamran took one of the armchairs in front of the desk. He folded his hands to keep them from trembling.

Tasman looked at a paper on his desk, then up at Kamran. "I asked you to stop by because of the situation with your father and your brother. The police were here earlier."

Kamran paused for a couple of beats, then asked, because he couldn't think of anything else to say, "Were they looking for me?"

"Well, they came to ask about you, background information. As chairman of student affairs, I handle special situations like this, you understand."

"Yes, sir."

"Anyway, they asked about your classes, how you are doing, your attendance record, whether you've missed any classes. Mrs. Rahat called up your files and printed them out. They showed you have missed just four days in the last three years. According to the database, that's the third-best attendance record in the law school." Tasman settled back in his chair. "They also asked about your friends and the people you associate with. I could only tell them that you are well liked by students and faculty. Mrs. Rahat printed out your personnel file. It showed you have no disciplinary actions against your name. Nothing."

Kamran was starting to sweat.

"I'm happy to tell you that both of the officers left here very impressed with you as a solid citizen and an outstanding student." Tasman looked again at the paper on his desk. "I guess you know Geo News is running a picture of your brother. Dani, is it?"

"Yes, sir."

"They are also giving out his name. Of course the dean and the board are not happy about this kind of publicity, even if it only tangentially involves one of our own."

Kamran could feel the sweat in his armpits. "I understand, Dr. Tasman."

"You're here on a full scholarship, aren't you?"

"That's correct."

Tasman nodded. "Quite an achievement. I helped design the scholarship test, and I know how difficult it was to pass."

Kamran could not hold back any longer. "Sir, am I being kicked out of school?"

Tasman held up a hand. "No, no. Nothing like that. In fact, the dean and I want you to know how much we prize students of your caliber. You've been handed nothing, taken nothing for granted. Your professors are on record with high evaluations across the board. Professor Qasim says you're among the sharpest law students he's ever taught. You've earned your place at this university."

Kamran wiped sweat from his brow.

"The dean and I, and the board, want you to know we're on your side. Your family is experiencing a time of trouble. That's to be regretted, but we stand by you."

"I can't tell you how relieved I am, Dr. Tasman. Frankly, I thought—"

"That we'd turn on one of our own? Why should we? You're accused of nothing. What have you done? Nothing. This is a school dedicated to independent thinking and high academic standards. But there are also moral standards. You have our vote of confidence, Kamran. We believe in you."

Kamran had to get out of Dr. Tasman's office quickly because he was on the verge of losing it. Zain was waiting for him on the steps of the admin building. "Well, what did Tasman have to say?'

"He said a lot of things. But the bottom line is, I'm not going to be kicked out of school."

"See, I told you to relax. Come on, let's head over to Anarkali."

Kamran's mind was spinning wildly with a mixture of anxiety and relief. "If you don't mind, I'd like to stop by the student mosque for a few minutes."

FOURTEEN

Men love their country, not because it is great,
but because it is their own.

SENECA

Zalman Khan was pacing the interrogation room when Awais was brought in. "Good afternoon," the lawyer said and pulled out a chair for his client.

Awais sat down. He was clear-eyed and alert, though the prison suit gave him a woebegone, run-to-ground look. "I didn't expect to see you again so soon, Zalman."

"There have been developments, Mr. Reza. I need to bring you up-to-date."

"Have you spoken with Shez?"

"I have, sir. She's holding up well, considering. I gave her your message. She sends her love in return, and so do Sallu and Kami. They miss you very much and are saying special prayers every day."

"They won't let anyone visit me. There's a fellow in here for killing his cousin because she refused to have children. Stabbed her fifty times. He gets visitors every day."

"Your case is different than a homicide, Mr. Reza. As I've said before, these are charges involving state security. That makes it as serious as something like espionage. Possibly more serious, given the recent attacks by extremists. And we've talked about the political pressure from abroad. The foreigners are breathing down the neck, as they say, of the big shots in Islamabad. They're demanding action against the Taliban and associates—preferably with a high body count. This is what we're dealing with, Awais. Your case is seen as a level-one counterterror matter. That's why no visitors."

Awais listened, barely reacting. "What are these developments?"

Khan folded his hands on the table and looked at his client. "I have to tell you, I've learned some things about your son."

This brought Awais to full attention.

"The prosecutor spoke with me this morning and gave me a few details. The truth is, Awais, Dani is part of a group of Pakistani Taliban. A counterterror unit tracked them down to a house outside Lahore. There was a shootout, and a number of soldiers were killed. Apparently there were guards hidden on the approach to the safe house. They ambushed the soldiers when they tried to raid the place. Dani and the others got away. During their escape, they killed some more soldiers and shot down a military helicopter. According to the prosecutor, the army took a real beating."

Awais slowly lifted his head. "My *God*," he gasped. He looked into the air and back into the misty past with incredulous memory. "I was myself in such shootouts in Bangladesh. And now my own . . . "

"From what I understand, the team Dani is part of is led by a maniac of a warlord, an amir named Gul Nawaz. It seems he was one of the key planners of the shrine bombing."

"My son, my son," Awais whispered helplessly.

"I'm sorry about this, Awais. But the prosecutor is being truthful with me. Dani is a terrorist, and there will be no saving him. They are already running pictures of him on the TV news. They give his name—and yours." Khan rubbed his face. "Look, this man Nawaz is bloodthirsty and is known to be the trainer of suicide bombers. Dani is one of them."

Now Awais looked sick, as if he were going to vomit. "No, no, no, no."

"I know this comes as a shock, but there it is. I knew you had to be told. They're looking for the whole Nawaz gang. They will shoot to kill. That makes your case much more difficult. Since you insist on going to trial, they are transferring you to another holding facility."

Awais was groggy with shock. "Where is this?"

"Islamabad, I'm afraid. They have a special prison there for terror cases." Khan put his hand on Awais's arm. "My friend, won't you reconsider the two-year deal I've worked out for you?"

Awais looked at the lawyer and then away. "You are a good man, Zalman. You are a wise and able lawyer. And I thank you for all you are doing on my behalf. But nothing has changed, because I am still myself. I cannot escape my own fate. If Allah means for me to die in prison, what chance have I to prevent it? My wife thinks our fate is composed in the stars. Allah has written it there. I don't necessarily believe in that, but I do believe in being true to my own values. For what am I but the sum of my values? No, Zalman, I will not plead guilty to anything I have not done. If my son has chosen the path of violence and destruction, it is Allah's will, not mine."

When Awais fell silent, the lawyer continued to watch him. "Mr. Reza, you have a hard shell. I can't say I'm surprised. I was looking over the trial papers from years ago when the army had you up on charges. They had no evidence against you and the other men. But I was interested in this story about you and the others *walking* from a POW camp in Bangladesh across India and home to Pakistan. That's incredible. That's over fifteen hundred kilometers. How long did it take?"

"Five months and a few days. We had to go slowly and keep out of sight."

"You've been through a lot in your life. I guess you're taking this situation as just another event in an eventful life."

"No," Awais corrected, "I'm taking it as the *worst* event in an eventful life."

∽∞∾

IN ANARKALI, Shez was getting ready to go to work at the hospital. She still felt sick and had no appetite but forced herself to swallow a little soup just to put something in her stomach. The sick feeling was reminiscent of those months back in 1972 when Awais had been missing, his fate unknown. It all came back to her in vivid detail: the report from the Red Crescent that he had been killed in battle. It had been a time of indescribable anguish despite the comfort of family, friends, and neighbors. And then, when it came to her that he wasn't dead, there had been a secret rejoicing, shared only with Awais's mother. And when Allah had answered her prayers, the rejoicing had turned into a deepening faith. Now her husband was in trouble again, and it was once more her faith that she depended on for that essential commodity, hope.

Still, it was all she could do to keep going through the motions of everyday life. She had to will herself to keep up an appearance of normalcy. She had to do it for Awais and the children. They couldn't be allowed to see her hidden despair. Allah would know of her great devotion since girlhood and whether she was deemed to be among the deserving ones, He would come to her aid, as He had always done. That was now all she could cling to.

Shez checked the clock. There was still half an hour before the pickup van from the hospital would arrive. She put on the TV and tuned in to her favorite soap opera, then hardly paid attention to it.

In a while, Salman walked in. "Hello, Ammi."

"Salman, you're home very early."

"There is no business. The Anarkali bazaar is as quiet as a camel's mind."

Shez left the television and went into the kitchen. "I have some fresh tea on the stove."

Salman sat at the table. He did not look quite right. He was dry-mouthed and blinked too much. "You're working tonight?"

"Yes," she called from the kitchen. "The ICU and the step-down unit are very busy."

"How are you feeling, Ammi?"

She brought in two cups of hot tea and sat down at the table with him. "I'm feeling better now that I know he's coming home. When do you think they'll let him out?"

"The lawyer said it can take a few days. The money is paid, and everything is all set. We just have to be patient. It'll happen soon."

Shez was watching her son. "You don't look well, Sallu. Is something wrong?"

He drank the tea and did not look at her. Finally he said, "I do have something to tell you. It's not great news."

Shez sat up, alarmed. "From the lawyer?"

Salman shook his head. "No, it's something else. Kami called. He told me to watch the early news. So . . . "

"Go on."

"Well . . . they've just released pictures of the suspects in the shrine bombing. Dani's one of them."

Shez slowly put down her teacup, a controlled and careful movement, as if she were afraid of coming unglued and didn't dare move much. "The shrine?" she croaked

"There's a little more, Ammi. Should I tell you now?"

"Please."

"They're running Abba's picture and his name. He is called a 'suspect.'"

Shez's mouth opened and moved up and down, but nothing came out for a moment. "A suspect in the bombing?" she managed to say.

"Yes. It's crazy! I spoke to Zalman Khan, and he's trying to get the newspeople to pull Abba's picture." He gulped and choked. "There's nothing we can do about Dani. They have all kinds of evidence against him."

It was welling up in her now, but she couldn't let go, not in front of her child. "Oh, Dani . . . " she whispered. It sounded like the breath of a ghost.

Salman was red-eyed and quiet.

"I don't understand," she said. "How can they say Awais was involved in something that he had nothing to do with?"

"The lawyer told me that even the prosecutor admitted they had no real evidence against him. Just that one thing about him giving money to Dani when that gunman was with him that time in the shop. I talked to him for a few minutes while Dani was in back with Abba. There was no 'terrorist meeting.'"

"But what about the money we paid?" Shez asked.

"Nothing's changed, according to Zalman. Abba will soon be given a small bond, and once we pay that, he'll be released. Are you sure you're up to going to work tonight?"

"I have to. They need me at the hospital. Besides, I have to be doing something." She looked at her watch, then got up, went to the window, and looked into the alley. "The van should have been here by now."

Salman watched his mother move aimlessly about the room, into the kitchen, and back again. Pouring more tea, sitting down. She was restless and more than a little unnerved. Her son had no soothing words to offer. He had run out of words of comfort and didn't much believe in them anymore.

Ten minutes later, they watched the news together.

"Are you sure you want to watch, Ammi? I wanted you to hear it from me, but I don't think you should—"

"My husband? My son? I want to see what they have made of them!"

But this time the news was all about a politically active ex–soccer star who was making a name for himself by criticizing the Zardari administration, which was always easy to do.

Shez went to the window for the third time, then looked at her watch. "The van is never late."

"They probably ran into a security check. The traffic can really back up."

"No, the hospital has special permits that allow us to get ahead of the line. I'd better ring the nurses' station." Shez took out her mobile phone and made the call.

Salman kept the news on, hoping the channel had decided to drop the pictures. He didn't want her to see them. It would make him cry. When he looked again at his mother, she was putting down her cell phone with an expression he'd never seen before. "What's wrong?"

She sat in a chair and looked into space. "I've been suspended from working at the hospital. After all these years, I'm told not to come in."

∽

ANOTHER FEATURE OF the deluxe safe house was its underground garage. It had cost the owner over $1 million U.S., or rather cost the

Punjab state that much, since it had been built by convict labor siphoned off from the minimum-security prison in Lahore. Working the phones and on the computer for hours at a clip, Gul Nawaz had ordered four special vehicles, and his lieutenants had been quick to supply them. These were now hidden from sight.

The amir called Daniyal, Raj, and Nasir into the television room, where he filled them in on the situation with the use of a field map.

"We are essentially surrounded by soldiers. They are convinced that we are still in the area. Which we are, but we are not, as you can see, hiding in the forest or in a cave somewhere."

"Thanks it is, I guess." Daniyal murmured.

"According to the latest intelligence from our people, units of the Fourth Infantry are combing the fields and farmhouses all over this eastern area here on the map. But we happen to be situated way over here to the west. What's more, this is the estate of a powerful official, a man far above reproach or even suspicion. The soldiers will not dare come near here."

The amir was summoned away to take a call, leaving the three young men momentarily alone.

Raj pressed his palms together. "We are nearing the time of jihad," he stated with priestly simplicity. The three of them looked upon each other; the fearsomeness of holy work visible to them all. It was a time to reaffirm that they were brothers in blood. As had become their custom, they reached out together and formed a three-handed clasp, silently bowing their heads.

When Nawaz returned, he picked up where he'd left off. "Our targets are in Lahore, and we can reach them in a short time. So we will operate out of here until we are ready to act. I have decided to again use my old ruse of dressing in the attire of our enemies. So, my friends, we will all be playing soldier once again."

The three were pleased.

"Yes! When we are ready to strike, we will depart dressed as regular Pakistani soldiers. We will be in cars actually belonging to the Pakistani army. With the insignias on the vehicles, your false photo ID cards, and ranking chevrons, we will blend in with any units that might be lingering in the area. And we will not be challenged at a checkpoint. But there is a further advantage. Once we are in position and ready to strike, the uniforms we wear will serve as the perfect cover. Soldiers are allowed to come and go as they please, no? This we will use to our advantage."

"Brilliant, Amir, brilliant!" Nasir exclaimed.

Nawaz's lazy eye moved daringly. "I take my tactics from the rugged brothers. This is why I have never failed in any objective. The shrine was difficult due to the thick walls, but we discovered the weak points of the structure. The result is one of our most glorious achievements."

Raj spoke up and reminded the amir that he had been interrupted during the military raid and had so far revealed only two of the three targets.

"I have not forgotten. No, indeed. To the shopping plaza and the police building we add a third worthy target—a place where the swine send their offspring to be educated. A place where the arrogance of the West is worshipped over the word of God."

"A school," Nasir blurted out.

"Yes, but more than a mere school."

The amir turned to the TV screen with a remote control. Already queued up was video footage of a wide, urban campus area with students and faculty moving about. As with the other targets, these images had been captured by a pedestrian with a hidden camera.

"This is a school, yes, but a school of legal training. A law college. That makes it one of the incubators of the corrupt and ungodly." Now the images shifted to a large lounge area. "This is the

Student Center, which includes a big cafeteria. The whole building is insultingly Western in design, all glass and ugly cement slabs. No respect for the grand Muslim architectural traditions. Every day, this Student Center is filled with hundreds of our future 'elites,' if I may use the term for such filth. To eliminate them from the ranks of our enemies will be a stab to the heart of those who dare to question the ultimate power of Allah."

Daniyal drew in a sharp breath. "That college, Amir . . . my brother goes there. He is another of the false believers."

"Than you shall have the honor, my son," Nawaz muttered.

Daniyal closed his eyes. "Allah's will must be done."

FIFTEEN

We all know the epicentre of terrorism in the world
today is Pakistan. The world community has to
come to grips with this harsh reality.

MANMOHAN SINGH

Kamran was in his dorm room working on his laptop when he
got a call from Rania. She was using her friend's mobile so
that his number wouldn't show up on her bill for her parents
to see. "Why don't you answer my e-mails?" she demanded.

"Rania, I promised your father I wouldn't try to communicate
with you, even by e-mail. I promised."

"I know. He told me. Listen, dear one, my guardian angel is getting the car serviced. Nobody's watching me. Let's meet in the park
in fifteen minutes."

"But Rania—"

"No one will know. The car won't be ready for two more hours. He thinks I've got classes."

"I don't know, Rania."

"I'll be there. You know the spot," she said and hung up.

It wasn't like Kamran to go back on his word. Awais Reza had taught his sons the value of keeping a promise. "It's not just a matter of ethics; it's worth money," the old merchant had always preached. But wasn't this a very different matter? If no one knew they were meeting, would it really be the end of the world? Wouldn't it be worse to turn Rania away, the woman he loved, than to cheat a little on his promise to her father?

He left his dormitory and cut across the main plaza, heading for the large park a few blocks from the campus. At one point, Kamran happened to glance over his shoulder and saw that he was being followed. It was the same heavy-set Islamist who had pushed him down and made threats.

Quickly changing course away from the park, he cut into a portico that ran along the concourse and hid in the dense shadow of a square pillar. When the beefy man reached the portico, Kamran stepped into the sunlight, startling him. "Why are you following me?" he demanded.

The man sputtered and threw up his hands. "Hold on! I'm not following you. I heard about your brother Dani on the news. I just wanted to say, may Allah be with him." With that, he turned and walked away.

Kamran watched until the man was out of sight before he resumed his way to the park.

It was a sprawling place of wide lawns, bike paths, duck ponds, and quaint wooden bridges, cloaked by a tall forest of thick Himalayan cedars. The park was full of nooks and crannies where couples could be sure of privacy. Kamran and Rania had a secret spot in the woods that they called their "green room" because of the wide-spreading evergreen boughs that provided a snug hideaway.

Rania was waiting for him, looking wonderful in jeans and a long blouse. When she heard his approach through the undergrowth, she ran to him. They embraced—the first time they'd ever really held each other. Rania finally pulled away and sat down in a patch of grass, leaning back against a solid old tree. He sat next to her and began to pick at blades of grass.

"How are you doing?" he asked.

"What do you think? How about you?"

He sighed. "I think about you all the time."

She smiled. "I saw Zain in the library this morning. He told me about your meeting with Dr. Tasman."

"That's about the only good thing that's happened lately. I guess you heard they've got my father's and Dani's pictures on the news. They're both accused of being in on the explosions at the shrine."

Rania shook her head in disgust. "That's insane. Your father a terrorist!"

Kamran continued to pluck at the grass. "The lawyer says they've got evidence against Dani but nothing really on my father. Let's not talk about it."

"Let's not. Look, the reason I wanted to see you . . . my mother is after me again to marry her friend's son. The one I told you about. Of course I absolutely refused, for the tenth time. That's nothing new. But now my parents want to send me to England to finish school."

Kamran's heart sank. "England? Isn't that a big island somewhere?"

She smirked. "This is serious, Kami. I may have to go."

He stopped picking at the grass. "I see."

"Ever since my father talked to you, my mother has been working on him, pestering him to send me away from Pakistan. It's too dangerous here, she's saying."

"It is."

"All right, it's dangerous," she said. "It's dangerous for everyone, not just me. What kind of country would this be if we all just up and moved out?"

Kamran nodded. "What did you mean, you may have to go?"

"My father is making a special order out of it. He thinks there are too many things going on around me. You, the terrorists, the police crackdown, the way the country is going. He's given me kind of an ultimatum. He's insisting I drop out of school here and get my degree in England. That's not what I want, Kami. But he's insisting."

Kamran stood up restlessly and stretched his legs. The woods were quiet, the only sounds flittering birds and the distant hum of city traffic. "Whatever you decide to do, I'll support you."

Now Rania stood and walked around the patch of grass; she had the look of a lost child who is just realizing she's lost. "I've always said Allah is testing our love. But something tells me that if I go to England . . . it'll be the end of us."

"Not if I have any say in the matter, my darling girl." He moved over to stand next to her. "Always remember, whatever happens, wherever you are, I will not forsake you."

⟡

AT THE ANARKALI BAZAAR, Salman looked out of the shop at the still thin numbers of people browsing in the bazaar. Just before nightfall, a well-dressed woman and her brother wandered in and looked around. Salman was solicitous and polite, and the woman ate it up. She finally bought a bolt of expensive chambray cloth, which made the whole day profitable. Business was way down, but the recent big spenders were keeping business afloat. Allah was indeed watching over the troubled Reza clan.

Salman stayed open later than he'd been doing lately but sold only a few trifles. When Noor shut his mobile-phone shop and came by, Salman also closed up, and they retired to the back room to sit for a while. It had become a regular routine. After-hours tea and opium relieved the stresses and frustrations of the day.

"My cousin just got back from his third trip to New York," Noor said. "He says opium has become popular with the elites, when they can get it."

"From what I've heard, you can get anything in New York. How's business?"

Noor snorted. "What business? I sold two phones and a calling plan all day."

While Salman was packing the little pipe with a chunk of opium, the electricity sputtered and went off. Reflexively, he lit the large candle kept handy on the sideboard for the daily load-shedding. They passed the opium pipe back and forth in the candlelight.

"Gives new meaning to the term 'dark ages,'" Noor cracked.

"As Abba always says, this is how we live now."

"Excuse me for being nosy, Sallu, but may I ask how much you have paid to get Awais out on bond?"

"Just between us and the goat outside, one hundred thousand rupees."

Noor whistled. "That's over a thousand U.S."

Salman told him about the married couple who had bought the silver tiara and the silver watch, the profit from the sale covering the bribe he'd paid that very same afternoon. "I am convinced it was the hand of God at work."

Noor took a long puff on the pipe. "There is no doubt, Sallu."

"Did you see their pictures on the news?"

"Dani and Awais? Yes, everyone has."

When Salman took his next turn with the pipe, he held in the fumes until he was red in the face, then exhaled slowly. "What are the other merchants saying?"

"That Awais is no terrorist. We've all known Awais for years. Your brother might have gotten mixed up with the wrong people at that madrassa, but that is not your father's doing. Dani is a grown man." Noor noticed the front page of the newspaper lying on the sideboard. "The foreigners are at it again with their attacks. Let's hope this time they kill the terrorists and not some poor family living in a hut."

"The Americans are supposed to be our allies," Salman said, his voice mellowed by the opium. "But what good does it do the average citizen of Pakistan? Things were bad enough before, but ever since the Yankees came, everything has gotten a lot worse."

"One hell of a lot worse." Noor sipped his tea and settled back in the chair. "How is your mother?"

It was getting warm in the cramped room, and Salman opened the back window. "She's just counting the hours until Abba can come home." He sighed. "Also, they've suspended her from the hospital."

"Because of those pictures on TV?"

Salman nodded sadly. "So now she feels humiliated, ashamed. It's all so stupid, the whole damn mess. She loved that job. It was her way of helping others, and now that's been taken away."

Noor took another hit off the pipe and put it down. "I guess she saw those pictures on the news, huh?"

"That's all she does now is sit there in front of the TV and wait for the news reports."

"She'll come to herself once Awais is free and back home."

"I just hope it happens soon. I don't know how much longer she can keep it together."

∞

AT THE POLICE holding facility in Lahore, Awais Reza was called out of his solitary cell before dawn.

"You're being transferred, Reza," the jailer muttered. "This way."

Awais was taken into a large waiting area where a dozen tired men were perched on beat-up wooden benches. It was a mix of the troubled, the forlorn, and the doomed. Awais sat down next to a prisoner who had a bloodstained bandage on his head. He leaned toward Awais. "Where are they taking us?"

"Islamabad, I think."

The man sank back and mumbled, "No one ever returns from Islamabad."

✂

BACK WHEN THE United States had been pounding the Taliban right after 9/11, when Osama bin Laden, with his lieutenants and fighters, had been forced to scurry from his Afghan strongholds into the mountainous regions of Pakistan, Gul Nawaz had vowed to take the fight to the infidel enemy. "They have come to destroy us," he had said. "But it is these crusaders who will die, their false gods who will be torn down."

He prided himself on being a soldier who fought hard and planned smart and was unafraid of trying unexpected maneuvers. Nawaz was a naturally devious specimen from a long line of peasants who had had to be devious in order to survive in the rugged Northwest Frontier Province. Once the U.S. military was on the ground in Afghanistan, there were so many freedom fighters willing to wage jihad that Nawaz had a ready supply of loyal fanatics. With financial backing from sources close to Iranian intelligence, Nawaz devised attacks that were extremely costly to U.S. and coalition forces.

In late 2003, Nawaz had prepped and dispatched a young shepherd turned suicide bomber into the area just over the border with

Afghanistan. In a godforsaken village that didn't even have an official name, coalition soldiers had set up a staging area for their raids
on known Taliban supply lines. The Yanks had made themselves at
home, erecting prefab huts and a large chow hall. The perimeter of
the village was fortified with armored guard posts manned around
the clock. Nawaz had learned from an encrypted e-mail from his
superiors that the foreigners had made friends with the local people,
handing out food supplies and sweets for the children. The message
explained that the local people had a tradition of holding an open
market in the center of the village each weekend. This drew hill
people from surrounding villages as well as the foreign soldiers who
were anxious to befriend the locals. Farmers, merchants, and crafts-
men would set up their makeshift stalls and sell their products until
evening prayers. As a show of friendship, the foreigners had handed
out dozens of large Coleman coolers for those bringing goods to the
market.

Gul Nawaz seized on this detail.

The shepherd boy was equipped with four of the coolers. Using
a sturdy donkey to carry the heavy load, he made his way early that
weekend morning up a certain hillside trail that few knew about.
As instructed by Nawaz, the shepherd timed his arrival in the village with the arrival of other tradesmen coming from nearby communities. It was easy to blend into the scores of goods sellers, many
with the distinctive Coleman coolers on donkeys or lugged by hand.
There was a simple security checkpoint, and the shepherd joined
others as they lined up and moved past the soldiers. The checkpoint
offered inspection; there had never previously been any trouble from
the stallholders or marketeers. Market day was something of a holiday. When the shepherd came to the soldiers, he was asked to open
the lids on his coolers, which he did with a smile. They were packed

with all kinds of miscellaneous merchandise—cosmetics and toys, canned goods and soaps, cooking oil and dried fruit. One cooler was packed with American books. The soldiers passed the shepherd through.

Several hundred people in the village center were milling about the various vendors. The shepherd unpacked his donkey and set up his coolers within sight of the soldiers' chow hall. During the next few hours, he sold numerous items to the villagers and those in uniform, exchanging pleasantries as he did so. At some point, when the hot sun was high in the sky, the chow hall began to fill up with hungry soldiers. Some of the tradesmen carried their coolers to the chow hall and began hawking items to those standing in line for their meal.

The shepherd waited for his opportunity. When he saw that the hall was crowded, he picked up the heavy cooler with the dozens of books in English, mostly paperbacks, and made his way inside.

The blast from the plastique secreted in the air pockets of the cooler could be heard echoing in the mountains for miles around. Eleven coalition soldiers were killed and another forty badly injured. The explosion also killed ten villagers in the market. None of the investigators who later came to pick over the bloody debris ever learned the identity of the shepherd.

For this unusual and intimidating strike against the enemy on his own turf, Gul Nawaz was elevated in the ranks of insurgent operatives and given more power and access to funds. Over the next couple of years, he designed and executed several more attacks against Western forces and interests.

His legendary reputation was made after an incident on Pakistani home soil, in Karachi in 2005. Nawaz had been summoned to a meeting in a downtown hotel. Present were Taliban military commanders, aides to Osama bin Laden, and their contact man from Tehran. As the group of extremists sat in the comfortable suite and discussed their plans and ideas for defeating the infidels, a squad of Pakistani soldiers slipped into the hotel and up to the floor where the men were assembled. They had a passkey and positioned themselves at the door. With stubby machine guns cocked, the door was thrown open. The soldiers rushed into the suite.

Gul Nawaz dove behind a heavy desk and drew his Russian 9-mm. The soldiers began shooting, dropping men in their seats who had not had time to unholster their pistols. Keeping low, Nawaz leaned out from behind the desk and fired back. His aim was deadly, and the soldiers fell as they were hit. Seeing a path to the open door, Nawaz rammed a fresh magazine home and rushed from behind the desk.

A wounded soldier lying on the floor managed to lift his weapon and get off a single shot before dying. The bullet ricocheted off a wall, then glanced off Nawaz's eye socket. But he kept going for the door and out into the hall. He was half blinded by the blood flowing from his wound, but he spotted another man just beyond the door frame. Nawaz fired from the hip, and the soldier staggered back, dropping his weapon. Nawaz moved fast for the stairwell door, but the soldier lunged back at him with a black knife.

As Nawaz whirled around, the soldier slashed the knife hard across Nawaz's chest, through his shirt and deep into the flesh. Nawaz shot him in the forehead and made it through the stairwell door.

Bleeding from his chest and from around his eye, Gul Nawaz got to a back alley and used his mobile to call an aide. He hid himself in piles of garbage until he was rescued and driven to a trusted doctor. Nawaz spent a week recovering at a safe house before he could safely move back to the border lands. He had a nasty scar on his chest and had permanently lost muscle control in one eye, but his reputation for fearlessness was assured.

He gave thanks to Allah for these marks of devotion. In the years to come, Nawaz would use his wounds as a badge of eminence, his lazy eye an unforgettable reminder to all of just whom they were dealing with.

SIXTEEN

If your house is burning,
wouldn't you try and put out the fire?

IMRAN KHAN

At the police facility in Lahore, the prisoners had been sitting
on the wooden benches in the hot, windowless room for
more than four hours. No one came to say when they would
be moved or what the holdup might be, or even when they would be
given something to eat.

"We're trash," one man sounded off disgustedly. "They won't
tell us anything but sit and wait. What the hell are we going to do
about it?"

"Even the blasphemous are allowed to eat," another put in.

Awais kept to himself and did not join in as the others complained. From the general chatter, he could tell that some of the
prisoners were hardened street criminals proud of their profession,

while most of the others claimed to be innocent of whatever wrong-doing they were accused of. That was easy to believe.

Awais did not look particularly annoyed, just tired and uncomfortable in the heat of the closed space. He sat inertly, looking at nothing, expending no energy, as if he'd given himself up as a lost cause and was ready to accept his fate.

A man next to him with a bandage on his head asked, "Have they let your family visit?"

Awais shook his head.

"That's not right. When they transfer you for trial, they have to let you have a visit. Know why? Because they must prove to the family that you're not dead and they're not just saying they're transferring you to cover it up."

There was a clanking as the door was unlocked. A jailer with a clipboard of papers came in and had the men line up in a single file. "The bus has arrived. You will file out one at a time, go to the end of the hall and out into the compound. Let's go!"

Everyone assumed they would be driven the long distance to Islamabad by bus. However, once they had boarded the rickety old bus and settled into the battered seats, two armed guards joined the driver, and from their conversation, it was clear that they were on their way to Lahore's main airport, a short distance outside the city.

Awais had a window seat and watched as the bus hissed and groaned its way out of the police lot and into the street. Ahead was a security checkpoint manned by soldiers, but the bus was waved on through without stopping.

The lead guard, a frisky fat man, stood near the driver and called for attention. "When we get to the airport, you will get off the bus and form a single line. We will be boarding a military plane, and there will be armed guards watching you. They are authorized to shoot if the need arises. You will file into the plane and take a seat. No talking, no stepping out of line."

"Sir?" someone called out. "Will we get something to eat on the plane?"

"This isn't a holiday trip. You'll eat when you get to the lockup in Islamabad."

The rest of the bus ride was grim—hot and uncomfortable, like a slow-motion journey toward the end of the world. Awais Reza watched as they passed through a shabby suburb and then onto a six-lane motorway. His expression remained blank, empty. He wasn't even thinking about anything. That was best. He had learned a long time ago in Bangladesh that sometimes it could help not to think about anything. His wife, his children, his business, his life—for now, he would think of none of it.

Sprawling Allama Iqbal International Airport was jammed with vehicles trying to get to the various terminals. The decrepit bus took a separate access road and trundled to the far end of a runway. An old twin-engine prop plane with Pakistani army markings sat waiting. A squad of soldiers and fliers milled around on the tarmac. The bus pulled up and stopped at the side of the runway. The doors creaked open, and the prisoners were ordered out.

It was a hot afternoon, and the humidity was high. The hungry men felt limp and wilted. Awais was perspiring heavily, his jail uniform stuck to his back, yet he held himself as erect as the young lance corporal had once held himself after the humiliating defeat at Dacca. There was a perverse pride in his manner, courage displayed at the brink of oblivion.

They were forced to stand in the bright heat while the plane crew finished their preparations. Twenty minutes went by before the boarding steps were finally wheeled into place.

The fat guard took a stance at the head of the line. "We will now board the plane. No talking, no stepping out of line. Ready? Move out!"

As the men filed up the steps and into the plane, a jeep of the Metro Police came racing off the access road and pulled onto the tarmac. Two men got out of the jeep, one in a police uniform and the other in a suit and tie. Awais recognized his lawyer, Khan.

"Hold it up!" the policeman called. He stepped over and talked to the head guard.

Zalman Khan looked around, spotted Awais, and ran to him. "Mr. Reza, come on! You've been bonded out!"

Awais put a hand over his brow, pushing the sweat away, shading his eyes in the harsh sunlight. "Allah be praised," he mumbled.

Khan took Awais by the arm and pulled him out of the line. The other prisoners watched with envy as the two headed toward the jeep.

"I suspect more than Allah's hand is at work here," Awais said, managing a weak smile.

"We'll talk about that later," Khan said. "We have to—what's wrong?"

Awais stopped at the side of the jeep. His head wobbled and his arms flailed as he fell to the ground.

"Mr. Reza!"

∞

THERE WAS MUCH activity at the safe house Gul Nawaz and his men had taken over. Final preparations were being made as the time for jihad drew near.

Daniyal, Raj, and Nasir spent an hour trying on different-sized army uniforms, all of sergeant rank. They needed them to be loose enough to conceal the special items they would be wearing underneath.

Once they had each found the right uniform size, they were fitted for the nylon vests and thigh pockets. The vests were strapped to the midsection and around to the back, with shoulder straps to support the weight. The leg pockets went from knee to midthigh. For measurement purposes, bars of lead were used to fill the numerous compartments, simulating the bulk and weight of sculpted C-4 and the thin plates of steel that would fragment during the explosion, guaranteeing lethal damage over a wide area. Each man would be carrying over eleven kilos, some twenty-five pounds, of killing power under the uniform. The technical aide showed how he would thread the detonator wire through the pants pocket, where it would be attached to a microswitch.

They finally suited up for a full dress rehearsal. The three strapped on the heavy vests and leg attachments, then donned the army uniforms over it all. They paraded around and looked over one another. Nawaz said Raj and Nasir had the right appearance, nothing particularly bulky showing, easily able to handle a normal gait. But Daniyal's uniform was too small for him and had to be changed.

Later that night the trio was served another sumptuous meal by the inconspicuous house staff. Afterward Nawaz called everyone into the TV room.

"When we are about holy work, we must keep the focus on our objectives," he began with quiet passion, his lazy eye straying freely. "We must rid our minds of earthly matters and all personal concerns—for the kingdom of heaven awaits. We must focus single-mindedly on the path set for us."

As the three young men sat listening intently, Nawaz began his step-by-step instructions. "We will all leave here in uniform and in the three army vehicles we have in the garage, supplied by our military brothers in arms. You will each ride in a separate car driven by one of my aides. Each vehicle prominently displays a staff insignia. That means we can move past any checkpoint without stopping.

Central Lahore is only forty minutes from here, and we will arrive well before zero hour."

The amir went on to explain that each bomber would be dropped off a mile from his target. At that location, they would each find a parked motor scooter, the same ones they had practiced riding at the first safe house.

"So you see, you will have to do very little walking through the entire mission, most of that at the target site. You will each drive the scooter to your respective target at the appointed time," Nawaz said. "You know the streets by heart and what options you have. You will park the scooter as close as possible to the emergency entrance at each location. The bikes will be packed with an extra-heavy load of explosives. After your work is complete and the target has been struck, as police and emergency workers arrive, one of our agents will explode the scooter by mobile phone. Thus, we will have double strikes at three locations!"

This devious strategy was received with relish and admiration by the three martyrs-to-be.

"Each of you will have a separate time for your act. Raj, I start with you."

"Yes, Amir."

"You will have the pleasure of delivering the first blow at the shopping plaza food court."

Raj leaped to his feet. "I am humbled by this honor!"

Daniyal and Nasir hugged him with brotherly admiration.

Nawaz went into the details of how the explosion at the plaza should occur. "Our sightings show that the food court is most crowded at about 3:00 in the afternoon. Raj, you will be in place some minutes before then. You will position yourself centrally among the crowd. When your watch reaches 3:00, press the button in your pocket. Allah will be waiting for you with the arms of eternity."

Raj fell to his knees and began to silently pray.

"Nasir," the amir went on, "you will have the police building an hour later."

Nasir dropped to his knees, too emotional to speak.

Nawaz looked at the last man. "And you, Dani . . . you will have the glory of eliminating that pit of satanic teachings."

"The glory!" Daniyal gasped.

∞

KAMRAN HAD LOOKED FORWARD to at least seeing Rania in the two classes they shared, but on this day she was absent from both, which was rare for her.

He pretended to take no notice, but it threw him off, and he had trouble paying attention the lectures. When they had met in the park, Rania had talked about her father sending her away to England. But she had clearly said that if she was forced to go, it wouldn't be in the middle of the semester. Was it possible that her worried father had made her depart already? If so, she surely would have sent him a farewell e-mail. They had agreed that, should she go, they would keep in touch by e-mail and video chat. It wasn't the same as being together, but it would be better than nothing.

There was definitely something odd about Rania's absence from school. He couldn't call her mobile after having promised her father he wouldn't. That might even hasten the decision to send Rania away. Kamran kept checking his laptop for incoming e-mail, but there was nothing all day from her. He told himself Rania was just keeping to the promise they had made not to contact each other that way.

Back in his dorm later and feeling restless, Kamran lay down for a nap but had too much to think about to sleep. His brother was lost to violence; his father stood accused of high crimes; his mother was enduring her family's nightmare, dismissed from her beloved nursing position; the family's name was dishonored; and he was forced to endure a limitless separation from Rania.

After lunch, Zain dropped by, and Kamran was happy to have someone to talk to about Rania. "I don't like it that she's not in school. She never misses."

"So you think maybe her father went ahead and sent her off to England already? That doesn't sound right, Kam. You said she'd let you know if she had to suddenly leave the country."

"Maybe her father won't let her. Maybe he thinks I might try to stop her from going."

"She'd find a way to let you know."

"You'd think so." Kamran forced a goofy grin. "After all, according to her, I'm the 'apple of her eye.' I still don't understand that expression."

"She's fallen hard for you, Kam. I've seen the way she brightens up when she looks at you. There's no way she's going to go flying off to another country without letting you know, father or no father. And besides, just because she's missed a few classes doesn't mean she's gone anywhere. Maybe she caught a cold."

Kamran started pacing the room. "You're right. I'm projecting, getting ahead of myself. Let's not talk about romance. There's an election coming up in a few years. Whom are they going to run?"

Zain smirked. "At this point, with all the terror turmoil and the way the economy is going, almost any smiley face might be able to defeat the incumbents. Wheat prices have tripled since Zardari took office."

"In my opinion, as humble as it might be," Kamran said, "it won't matter who runs or who wins, the Pakistan People's Party or any of the others. The military is probably going to step in at some point and ignore the election results."

"For reasons of 'national security,'" Zain mocked.

Kamran threw up his hands. "Hey, who knows? If the military does take power, they probably won't do worse than the civil governments have."

"That's a good point," Zain said. "Maybe they can keep us out of the failed-state column a little longer."

"Somehow, some way, Pakistan has always managed to pull itself out of trouble."

"It's starting to look like the Islamists might be a way to go. You don't agree, and I don't like it much myself, but a lot of people do."

Kamran shook his head. "An Islamic government is the same thing as a police state. Like Stalin had going in Russia, like China, North Korea. Like the Taliban imposed on the Afghans—and like they want to impose here on us. Forget it. A moderate Muslim like you wouldn't want to live under the harshness of sharia law."

Zain shrugged. "If it was too harsh, no, I wouldn't approve of it. But there is a more moderate form of Islamic law."

"That's fine for the mosques but not for the ultimate power of the state. The fundamentalists cannot be trusted."

Zain laughed. "In Pakistan, what politician has ever really been trusted?"

Kamran's mobile rang, and he slipped it out of his pocket.

"That's probably Rania now," Zain said.

Kamran glanced at the caller ID, shook his head, and clicked the talk button. "Sallu, good to hear from—"

"Kami, listen," Salman interrupted urgently, "I just got a call from the lawyer. Abba has been let out of jail. But he had a stroke or something. He's in the hospital."

Kamran sagged.

"They don't know if he's going to make it."

"Does Ammi know?"

"Not yet. I'm headed home now," Salman said, raspy and anxious. "I'll meet you over at the hospital."

∽∽∽

ALL DAY A NERVOUS Shez cleaned the house, then broke off every half hour to watch the television news. It was an obsession, and she asked Allah to forgive her weakness.

It was a horror to see her own child publicly depicted as a dangerous killer; it was the ultimate heartbreak to have her honest and courageous husband accused of outrageous crimes. It was maddening! Treacherous! The Reza name had been dragged through the mud. Because one son was tainted, so was the head of the family. If they had only asked around, they would have learned that Awais had a golden reputation as a hardworking shopkeeper, a peaceful and civil man who hated the extremists infecting Pakistan. Awais involved in the bombing at the shrine! The very idea was bizarre, surreal.

Shez kept remembering the hard times of the past and how Allah had helped her get through them. She could feel God's presence now. It was certainly there when Dr. Tasman had told Kamran he would not be expelled.

Salman burst into the house. "Ammi!"

Shez jumped up from the sofa.

"It's Abba. He's been released from jail, but he's fallen ill. He's been taken to the hospital."

She stood motionless, as if she simply couldn't comprehend what her son was saying to her.

Salman took her arm. "Come on, I've got a taxi waiting."

SEVENTEEN

Terrorism is a big danger to Pakistan's independence.
We will fight this danger for the sake of independence
of Pakistan and will defeat it at all levels.

FORMER PRIME MINISTER SHAUKAT AZIZ

Kamran got a fast ride on Zain's scooter and arrived at the hospital before his mother and Salman. He hurried through a waiting room filled with an assortment of wounded humanity and headed straight for the elevators. He knew his way around from having visited his mother a few times over the years when she was working the nurses' station. On the intensive care floor, he spoke to the elderly nurse at the desk.

"My name is Reza, and my father has been admitted here. Can I find out how he's doing?"

She tapped the keyboard on her computer. "Yes, Mr. Reza. Please take a seat in the waiting room. I'll tell Dr. Mubarak you're here."

"Do you know how he's doing?"

"Sir, I'll have to let Dr. Mubarak speak with you."

Feeling numb, Kamran wandered blankly into the large waiting room. There were padded chairs lining three walls; worried-looking men and women were sitting around in silence or just whispering. There was a solemn, funereal quality to the scene. Kamran spotted a Coke machine in the corner and went over to it, digging coins out of his pocket. A man in a tan suit came in, looked around, and walked over to him.

"Are you Mr. Reza's son?"

"Yes, Doctor, I'm Kamran Reza. How is he?"

"Oh, I'm not Dr. Mubarak," the man said and stuck out his hand. "My name's Zalman Khan. I'm your father's lawyer."

Kamran gripped his hand tightly. "Oh, yes. Glad to meet you, sir. I know you've done a lot to help my father. How is he doing?"

"He's in surgery right now," the lawyer said.

"Surgery? So it's pretty serious, huh?"

"I don't know. But because it happened at the airport, an ambulance was there in a matter of minutes. That may have made a difference. Let's sit for a minute, Kamran. There's been a development in your father's case."

They took a pair of chairs over by the windows where no one was sitting.

"I've had another talk with the prosecutor," Khan said quietly. "He was the one who signed off on your father's bond." He dropped his voice even lower. "He knows we put out a few rupees to get the release, but that's business as usual, and he knows that too. At any rate, your father is out on bond, but he still faces serious charges and the prospect of a trial. You realize that."

Kamran nodded.

"I collected a number of statements from your father's neighbors and the other merchants at the Anarkali bazaar, character witnesses. I went over these with the prosecutor. There are at least ten people who said they would be willing to testify that Awais was strongly opposed to terrorism and always spoke of extremist violence as something that was destroying Pakistan."

"I wish the police had done that research in the first place," Kamran muttered.

"They didn't want to. They were using your father as a way to get at Daniyal. The prosecutor knows we'll make that point at trial. Add to that this long list of solid character witnesses I've got."

"Plus, there's no evidence against him," Kamran said

"I reminded the prosecutor that the only real evidence he has is Awais's admission that he gave Daniyal a small sum of money when an unknown man was with him. But that was a self-incriminating admission. Whatever judge we draw will probably rule it inadmissible on those grounds. And what is suspicious about a father giving his son a little money? In short, there's no possibility a jury is going to convict your father of anything, and the prosecutor realizes it."

"So where does that leave us?"

"The state hates to lose at trial, especially a high-profile one like this would be. I think there's a good chance that all charges will be dropped at some point. It's a matter of time and a little face-saving."

Kamran grabbed the lawyer's hand and shook it. "You're a genius."

"Your father is a good man. I'm happy to—"

Kamran looked over and saw Salman and his mother. He rushed to them.

"Any word?" Salman asked.

"He's in surgery, but they say he was treated quickly and has a good chance of pulling through."

"A good chance?" Shez shot back. "That's all? Just a *chance*?"

Before they could take seats, a doctor in operating-room scrubs came in and called out, "Is the Reza family here?"

Salman raised a hand. "That's us."

He was a tall, middle-aged man who introduced himself as Dr. Mubarak. "I've just come out of surgery. Your father had a stroke. His heart and areas of the brain were damaged, but we may be able to save him."

"What are his chances?" Shez blurted out.

The doctor hesitated a moment. "At this point, Mrs. Reza, it's about fifty-fifty."

∞

BEHIND THE SCENES, Zalman Khan's superiors at his Lahore law firm had taken a little more interest in Awais Reza's case than Khan was permitted to say. In the course of going through the police and legal paperwork, as well as Khan's batch of revealing testimonials from those who had known Awais for decades, the senior partners in the firm had concluded that the case was utterly baseless. From the arrest to the prosecutor's charging package, it was nothing but junk law enforcement—a common commodity in contemporary Pakistan. It was clear to all the lawyers that Awais Reza was no terrorist or terrorist supporter. It was ludicrous to lump this humble shopkeeper in with guerrilla operatives capable of mounting an attack like that on the shrine. Reza had been an honorable soldier for his country and had lived as a typical middle-class businessman, with middle-class values. He was a moderate Muslim, not an extremist. Besides, as one of the firm pointed out, "Reza doesn't have the kind of money that the nasties need. They'd have little use for an old man like him."

On the other hand, the lawyers could see that young Daniyal Reza had fallen under the influence of the radical imams at his madrassa and was actively taking part in their terror plans. Khan's investigation had turned up the information that Daniyal Reza had been estranged from his family for several years because of his hard-edged religious leanings. The two other Reza brothers were known to have little or no contact with Daniyal. Kamran's high marks in law school drew special notice from the firm's partners. "I like this young fellow," one of them said. "He's the future of our profession if Pakistan stands any chance for a decent legal system."

As far as the partners in the law firm were concerned, the case of Awais Reza was another example of the state going after the defenseless little guy so it could look as if it were hitting hard at Pakistan's free-ranging militants without actually having to take on the bully boys who knew how to shoot back.

"It's the same old tune. The bastards in Islamabad are playing to the bastards in Washington," the head of the firm stated categorically. "They're chewing up innocent Pakistani citizens to impress the Americans that they're tough on terror. That annoys the piss out of me! And I mean to do something about it."

With Awais out of jail and in the hospital, Zalman Khan was given his instructions and turned loose. Using the firm's extensive high-level media contacts, Khan talked up the Reza case as another instance of Islamabad's disregard for the democratic rights of Pakistanis in order to appease the Americans. As Khan told a vice president at a major broadcast news service, "When you know the details, it's one of those human tragedy stories that really gets your blood boiling." Delivered with the right amount of controlled anger, it was a neat come-on to whet the appetite of the news merchants. It did not take long for Khan to plant his information with key players within strategic print and broadcast outlets. The Zardari administration was disliked by much of the media, and journalists were always on the lookout for stories that played up the government's problems, corrupt practices, and ineffectualness. Thus, the lawyer's "human tragedy" spin on Awais Reza's story held natural appeal for editorial chiefs. The case had everything—an antigovernment component in the clumsy and overplayed way the counterterror dragnet was being conducted coupled with a thumb of the nose at the smart-ass Americans while presenting the average Pakistani as a victim of the state's wayward policies. It was the kind of story that investigative journalists fight over.

That evening, a few reports began to appear on television detailing Awais Reza's mistreatment at the hands of the authorities. Jailed on a highly questionable charge, with no hard evidence against him, Reza had been held incommunicado, his family unsure of his fate. The reports played up his background as a combat veteran, highlighting his larger-than-life thousand-mile walk across hostile India to return to his beloved Pakistan. The stories depicted Reza as a respected store owner at the important Anarkali bazaar. Reza had eventually been released on bond, but by then his condition had deteriorated to the point where his health had failed, and he was now hospitalized in critical condition. One reporter gave the impression that Reza had only been given bond to avoid official costs for his medical treatment. "The timing of his release just when Mr. Reza had a stroke," the reporter intoned, "leaves one aghast at the callous thriftiness of our law enforcement officials."

Other outlets picked up the story, and soon a number of channels were running reports on the Reza case and providing updates on the unfortunate man's health. A widely circulated sound bite declared, "Doctors have given Mr. Reza at best a fifty-fifty chance of surviving. Attending physician Dr. Mubarak had no comment when asked if Awais Reza's condition was caused by his treatment while in custody. Our prayers are with him and his family. A fund has been set up for Mr. Reza's legal defense and for his medical expenses."

EARLY PRAYER WAS ALWAYS an emotional time for Daniyal Reza, but this morning in the private mosque, it was extraordinary. His mind was now clear of all the clutter and unworthiness; he could see into every part of the real world and was enraged by what he saw. Allah's terrestrial palace had become monstrously overcrowded by the infidels, with their deviant lives and their discredited gods. It thrilled Daniyal to think of his awesome responsibility. Today he would finally step forward as a soldier for Allah. He would strike down all who offended His Holiness, all who dared to defy His commands. He would give all there was to give for the honor of serving the One True God.

After breakfast, Daniyal, Raj, and Nasir met alone for an hour of meditation. In their capacity as holy annihilators, they would go about their work on this apocalyptic day with deep reverence. Their utter joy at commencing jihad was held in check, as the amir had cautioned. "Soldiers do not waste energy before the battle."

Later in the morning, they solemnly entered the dressing room and removed their clothing. On the wall was a blown-up photo of dead children littering a dusty street. The caption read, "They Must Be Avenged!"

Several young men assisted as the three began strapping on the nylon vests and leg pockets, now wired and weighted with packs of C-4 explosives sandwiched between thin plates of steel. The army uniforms had been tailored and altered overnight. The insulated detonator wires had been sewn into the inside of the pants and connected to the microswitch that was taped into each right-hand trousers pocket. The technician showed them the use of the switch. "In order to prevent a premature detonation," he explained, "I have tightened the set screws. So you must press firmly on the button to activate the circuit." He took out a demonstration switch and had them all test the pressure needed to make the electrical connection that would explode all of the C-4 packed onto their bodies.

When they left the dressing room, Daniyal, Raj, and Nasir were walking bombs in the uniform of everyday soldiers.

In another part of the safe house, crisply attired as a Pakistani army colonel, Gul Nawaz was attending to last-minute business at his desk when he received a coded flash-traffic message over the secure intranet connection on his laptop. He ran it through the decoder and read with growing concern. "Ashram!" he called out.

His aide instantly appeared from the next room.

"Are our glorious freedom fighters ready?" Nawaz asked.

"Yes, Amir. They are standing by awaiting your instructions."

"And the vehicles?"

"All three Humvees are fueled and ready to roll. The scooters are all in place. We have run checks on all the radios and put in new batteries."

"Backup weapons?"

"Cleaned and loaded," Ashram replied. "Fresh magazines in each gun and extra ammo cases under the rear passenger seats."

"Very good." Nawaz looked at his multidial wristwatch. "We leave in twenty minutes. But first we must deal with a small problem. I've just learned that central command has discovered several e-mails from one of our house staff here to his brother in Karachi. They are discussing the $5 million they would be paid if they turned me in to the Americans—dead or alive."

The aide stiffened.

Nawaz held up a steady hand. "By the grace of Allah, they are only in the discussion stage of their betrayal." He rocked back and forth in his chair as if to some inner rhythm. "Have all four of the staff assemble in the side courtyard. Tell them I wish to thank them for their service."

"May I have the honor of punishing the guilty one?" Ashram asked.

"The *one*? You should know by now my methods. If one person in a group is involved in a plot, we must assume all are involved. And yes, Ashram, you have earned the right."

Nawaz went out into the hall and across to the outer room where his three suicide bombers were waiting. When they saw him, they stood at attention. In their uniforms, they were simply ordinary soldiers reporting for duty. There was nothing remarkable about any of them. The amir looked them over and nodded with pride.

"We have prepared well," he said. "And we have made our prayers to Allah. Now we begin jihad. Follow me."

They went down the hall and stopped at a high window that looked out over the vast property. Nawaz pointed to the small courtyard at the side of the main house. The four domestic servants who had cooked their meals and attended to their needs were standing there talking to one of Nawaz's aides.

The amir held up an index finger. "Honored ones, observe how we deal with those who would stand against us."

After some moments, the aide walked away as Ashram appeared behind the servants with a machine gun. One of them turned and reacted as Ashram's weapon spewed bullets into the four of them. The men fell in a tangled heap.

"Vengeance is best when it is swift," Nawaz remarked.

⚬⚬⚬

SHEZ, SALMAN, AND KAMRAN remained in the hospital's ICU waiting room until late that evening. About 10:00, Dr. Mubarak came in and explained that Awais was still under sedation and there was nothing new to report. "He's in critical condition, but he's stable as of now. I suggest you all go on home and get some sleep. If there's any change, you'll get a call."

They went home, exhausted, but their sleep was fitful. Early in the morning, they had a hasty and gloomy breakfast, then returned to the hospital. Salman sat with Shez, and Kamran paced around the waiting room aimlessly, as were a few others anticipating word about a loved one. By noon, with Awais still sedated and unconscious, Salman went down to the coffee shop to fetch some sandwiches.

The head of the nurses' station, who had been Shez's supervisor, came in and went to her. "Shez, my dear lady. Please know that your suffering is our suffering."

"Thank you," Shez whispered.

The nurse put an arm around her. "Your husband has the best care possible. You never worked the cardiac unit, so you don't know him, but Dr. Mubarak is one of the top heart specialists in the country. We also have one of the best neurosurgeons in the city on your husband's case."

Shez nodded numbly. "What is the survival rate for a man in his sixties?"

"That's hard to say. But I understand the medics were there very quickly when it happened. That was a great piece of luck."

"He has always had God's hand on his shoulder," Shez said.

"Surely Allah is watching over him. I have to get back to work." She patted Shez's hand. "Be strong, my friend."

When Salman appeared with a sack of sandwiches, he rushed over to Kamran. "I just saw a news clip on the TV down in the coffee shop. It was all about Abba. Like a three-minute piece. They're saying he was wrongly accused, and that brought on the stroke."

"I don't understand," Kamran said, puzzled. "Why are they singling him out?"

"I don't know." Salman looked over at his mother, who sat there listlessly. "Now he has to get better. He has to live. He has to."

EIGHTEEN

The Taliban's acts of cultural vandalism—
the most infamous being the destruction of
the giant Bamiyan Buddhas—had a devastating effect
on Afghan culture and the artistic scene.

KHALED HOSSEINI

In the late afternoon, with still no change in Awais's condition, Shez and her two sons went down to the lobby coffee shop for an early dinner.

"It was nice of Noor and his son to keep the store open for you," Shez commented.

"He's always been a good friend," Salman said. "Very supportive. He's recording those news reports they're running about Abba."

Shez was eating small bites, still with little appetite. "It'll be so good for him to see what they're saying now. I knew they would figure out he was wrongfully accused."

"Mr. Khan said they'll eventually have to drop the charges," Kamran said. "With these reports coming out, with the media on our side, it should speed things up."

"And it's growing," Salman said. "The Lahore papers have picked up the story."

They did not linger in the coffee shop and went right back up to the ICU floor. After they found seats together in the crowded waiting room, Kamran caught sight of Zain out in the hallway, signaling to him. "Excuse me a minute," he said.

Zain greeted him with a strong hug. "I had to come and see how you and your family are doing. Any change?"

"No, but the doctor seems more optimistic today."

"That's encouraging, Kam. I've been watching the news. It's like Awais is a symbol for everybody who's ever been—excuse my Swahili—fucked around with by the system." Zain inclined his head toward the elevators. "Can you spare five or ten minutes? Somebody wants to talk to you."

"Who is it?"

"Call it a surprise guest."

From the lobby, they took the rear exit into the parking lot. Zain's motor scooter was parked near the walkway. Rania was leaning against it.

"I'll go grab a tea while you guys talk," Zain said and went back into the building.

Rania stepped forward. "My darling," she said and wrapped her arms around him.

He held her tightly. "I've missed you."

"That goes double for me."

Kamran pulled back. "We'd better be cool. Somebody'll report us to the love police."

"I don't care anymore," she snapped. "How's Abba? They said on TV he was in critical condition."

"He still is, but so far he's holding his own. You weren't in class. I was worried you might have . . . "

"What? Flown off to London without telling you?" She gave him a tap on the cheek. "You're a bad boy for even thinking that."

Kamran looked around the parking lot. "Where's your bodyguard?"

"I told my folks I didn't need an armed escort. They weren't happy, but . . . "

"You missed a big history test."

"I know, but I had to take time out to deal with my parents."

"You're going against your father's wishes just seeing me," Kamran said.

She looked away. "I had a couple of big arguments with my father, and we never argue. I had a couple with my mother too, but we argue all the time. He's been pressing for the 'London option.' That's what he calls it. Finally I told him I'd rather go to New York than to England. Frankly speaking, I'm not a tremendous fan of the Brits. They're nice people and all, very smart, but a little toy-box kingdom and everyone with a title? Cute, but I don't know if I could handle it. I'd be an outsider."

"You'd fit in anywhere."

"And then my mother gets into it and starts pushing this arranged-marriage thing all over again. That was another shouting match. I know my father is only trying to keep me out of harm's way, away from all the hassles in this country. But I was born in Lahore and grew up here. Why should I leave when so many others can't? I chose the legal profession because I want to help my own people have a better life. I wouldn't feel right running away from trouble."

"So what happened after all these arguments?"

"I stayed in my room most of the time. I just refused to discuss school or marriage or you or anything. You know how stubborn I can be."

He grinned. "Yes, you can be very stubborn."

Rania smacked his arm. "I'm only stubborn when someone's trying to get me to do something I don't want to do. And I don't want to live abroad, and I don't want an arranged marriage."

Kamran looked down and saw that he was holding her hand.

"I let them know I'm through being treated like a child," Rania said.

"And? . . ."

"Remember how I said Allah was testing our love?"

He nodded. "Of course."

"I think we've passed that test. This morning my parents saw a couple of news clips about your father's situation. I think my mother cried. My father finally realized he was judging the situation without knowing what was true and what wasn't. He sees that Awais was treated very unfairly. My father feels that he owes you an apology. You know what I told him? I told him he'd be lucky to have a son-in-law like you. Know what he said?"

"That you were crazy? Gone funny in the head?"

Rania giggled. "No, silly. He wants to meet with you. And surprise, surprise—my mother is going along with the whole thing!"

"Are you saying what I think you're saying?"

"I'm saying they're going to let us get married," Rania replied. "My father wants to tell you himself."

Kamran beamed. For a moment at least, nothing else was more important than this.

"I know this isn't the best time for you, Kami. But the timing is exactly right for meeting my parents. Can you sneak off for an hour or so to the Student Center? They'll meet us there."

GUL NAWAZ HAD DESIGNED his "false flag" attack well. With the security crackdown in the wake of the shrine attack and the increased number of soldiers constantly seen in and around Lahore, it was easy for Nawaz's three military Humvees to move in and out of traffic, to pass through checkpoints, and generally to blend into the background. The average citizen was leery of encounters with the police, and especially with the military, so they avoided contact if at all possible. Nawaz had instructed the bombers to adopt a superior, standoffish manner at all times. "Do not look approachable."

Raj was the first of the three to be dropped off, a mile away from the shopping plaza. "Allah be with you," the driver said with intensity.

The young man was serene and calm. "And soon I will be with Him. See you in the next world."

He was in an industrial area along the outskirts of the city. It took only a few moments to walk half a block, then turn into a cobblestone alleyway behind a commercial laundry. The explosives-packed motor scooter was parked at the curb, and a man in traditional dress was sitting on a stoop close by. When he saw Raj, he got up and ambled away. The key was in the ignition. Raj eased his leg up and over the seat, carefully placing himself on the seat, feeling the extra weight and tight straps under his sergeant's uniform.

A map of the streets and side lanes that led to the plaza had been thoroughly memorized. If traffic was jammed in one place, he knew of several alternative ways to reach his destination. In the upper pocket of his tunic was a flawlessly forged military ID card and a pass showing that he was off duty and cleared to be out on personal business. He did not expect anyone to ask to see these credentials.

Near one of the big intersections, he ran into a line of vehicles held up at a police checkpoint. Raj easily maneuvered his scooter between the waiting cars, vans, and trucks. He slowed to nod at the policemen manning the stop, then gunned the motor and went ahead without waiting for an okay. The police were not interested in challenging the military.

Traffic was less sluggish for several blocks, and he reached the plaza without further delay. The facility consisted of a large open-air plaza surrounded on all sides by elegant shops, mostly popular clothing outlets and several large department stores. Raj took the main driveway and cruised into the parking area behind the buildings. He drove on until he reached the rear of the warehouse, a big store that faced the food court. There was a dock and a loading ramp with a parking area. As he had been instructed, Raj wedged his scooter into a corner beside the ramp, which left it almost hidden from view. When the emergency units arrived, they would have to park nearby.

As Raj dismounted, the explosives strapped underneath his uniform felt tight and constricting, but he forced himself to adopt a normal pace. When he passed through the gateway into the plaza, he looked at his watch: six minutes to go.

The plaza was filled with customers laden with shopping bags, wandering in and out of the various stores. Just as he had seen on the surveillance video, the food court was crowded with young people congregating at the scores of tables, with scattered music players issuing a mix of pop tunes amid the chatter and hubbub. The unnoticed soldier stood off to the side, watching. He saw how shamelessly the girls were mixing with the boys.

Raj glanced again at his watch. When he looked up, his face was fixed, his expression devoid of human warmth. He put his right hand into his pocket and started forward.

On a side street two blocks from the plaza, Gul Nawaz sat in the front passenger seat of a black Mercedes sedan, his aide Ashram at the wheel. In their army-officer uniforms and with the general staff medallion displayed on the hood, they were impervious to challenge or even close approach. They looked like what they were supposed to look like: ranking military men on official business. From their position, they could see the rear of the store and a portion of the shopping plaza.

Shortly, Nawaz looked at the dashboard clock, muttering, "Any moment now."

First came the ground-shaking concussion, followed half a second later by the heavy blast, a galloping roar that bounced off the clouds and echoed out into the streets. An expanding mushroom cloud of black smoke, glass, concrete, steel, and mixed debris rose over the plaza in fearsome dimensions.

"In Allah's name, we rejoice!" Ashram shouted.

"It is His will we serve," Nawaz said. "Blessed be our martyr Raj. This day will mark the end of many things that are wrong with Pakistan."

In less than ten minutes, the area behind the store was alive with police sirens and the singsong wailing of ambulances. People were running from the plaza, while others were running toward it. Chaos and alarm were everywhere.

They had a clear view of the loading ramp where Raj had parked the motor scooter. The rear of the store had sustained little damage. Nawaz opened the glove compartment and took out a Nokia phone. When the first hook-and-ladder unit rumbled to a stop, Nawaz flipped open the phone. "Give me the signal."

Ashram lifted a finger and paused as two more emergency units arrived on the scene. Finally he dropped his finger.

Nawaz pressed a button on the phone. A beat went by; then came a horrific explosion stretching out everywhere in streams of orange fire and speeding debris. The back of the store had been blown open, and twisted steel girders hung loose. The police cars and two ambulances no longer existed. Much of the firefighting apparatus was wrecked and, ironically, on fire.

∽

THE HUMVEE CARRYING Nasir arrived at the drop-off spot precisely on time. The driver warmly clasped his hand. "Go with Allah's blessing and the gratitude of His children."

Nasir walked across the street to an industrial park and spotted the motor scooter in the employee lot. The man guarding the bike was sitting next to it in a utility van. When he saw the soldier approaching, he gave a slight nod, started the van, and drove off.

Nasir lifted the scooter's seat and checked the large dispatch envelope in the storage console. Without delay, he mounted the bike, his movements stiff and deliberate. The key was in the ignition, and the well-tuned engine kicked over on the first stroke. No one paid the slightest attention to a lone rider leaving the parking lot and pulling out onto the highway.

Downtown Lahore was not far away, and Nasir kept a steady speed weaving in and around the afternoon traffic. He reached the target office building on schedule. As instructed, he parked the scooter on the street between cars, half a block from the police headquarters, which took up the whole ground floor of the building. The 4:00 P.M. shift change was under way, with uniformed police officers coming and going.

Moving slowly, Nasir dismounted and locked the ignition. He opened the seat compartment and removed the olive-colored envelope marked with military insignias. Nasir shook himself and loosened his muscles. He was all business now, concerned about nothing, worried about no one. The end was here. Nothing could stop him now.

Dispatch in hand like a messenger, Nasir started toward the lobby, which was packed with uniformed and plainclothes officers.

The black Mercedes staff car was parked only two blocks away. Gul Nawaz and his aide could see Nasir as he waded in among the policemen. The explosion came moments later, thunderously blowing out windows along with parts of the building facade, all of it raining out into the street and catching pedestrians in midstride.

"In His name we conquer!" Ashram exclaimed.

Great flames erupted from the building as some men staggered out to collapse on the street, bloody and torn.

"Let us move on to our last target," Nawaz said. "Abdulla will handle the scooter bomb when the time is right."

NINETEEN

Let us sink all our differences and stand united together
under the same banner under which we truly achieved
Pakistan and let us demonstrate once again that we can,
united, face all dangers in the cause of glory of Pakistan,
the glory that the Quaid-i-Azam envisaged for Pakistan.

FATIMAH JINNAH

S alman sat with his mother in the crowded but subdued ICU
waiting room, listening by earbud to a miniradio. At one point,
he leaned over and whispered, "They're still counting the dead
at the big shopping plaza, Ammi—but now there's been another
bombing."

Shez clamped a palm to her forehead. "My *God*, where?"

"The main police station downtown. They say it's the same gang
who were behind the shrine attack."

She shook her head, appalled. "Dani is one of them, isn't he?"

"That is what is said."

"I do not blame him entirely. Much of the blame goes to those so-called religious leaders. Criminals, really. Poisoning young minds to further their evil business! They twist the beauty of Islam and make it seem ugly, inhuman."

Salman looked down. "I wish I'd paid attention when Dani started going to that madrassa and getting so serious about Islam. But I was busy at the shop, and I thought it was just a normal interest in religion, a good thing. I had no idea they were feeding him all that nonsense about killing the infidels."

"It wasn't your fault. You're like your father and Kami. None of you are very religious. But I should have seen that Dani was going in the wrong direction. Actually, I did. But by then, he wasn't listening to anyone except that damned imam they arrested."

"Dani was coached by professionals," Salman said. "It's that simple, Ammi." He glanced at the wall clock. "What time did Dr. Mubarak say he'd see us?"

"He's overdue now."

"There was a new piece on the news about Abba and his condition. People care about him, Ammi."

"What did the news say about his condition?"

"The same. They played that cut of Dr. Mubarak saying there was a fifty-fifty chance of survival. But that was on TV a day and a half ago. One of the stations said they're going to have a press conference here at the hospital, downstairs."

Shez took a tissue from her purse and touched her eyes.

"Don't cry," he said. "The doctors are doing all they can."

"I know. And I know that Allah is watching over us. Look at how Rania's parents changed their minds overnight. I see Allah's hand at work."

"Plus, Kamran is a great fellow. After they meet him, get to know him a little, her parents will realize they made the right decision."

Shez looked up. "Think of it. I'll have grandchildren."

"And I'll be an uncle."

A nurse appeared and said Dr. Mubarak would see them next door in the private lounge. Shez went tense. "I have a strong feeling he is going to make it," she whispered.

"As you have said, Ammi, Allah is watching over the Reza family."

Salman escorted his mother through the hall and into the lounge. Shez took a seat and fell to praying quietly. Salman stood next to her, head bowed in his own thoughts and prayers.

Soon afterward, Dr. Mubarak entered. He had on scrubs and looked sweaty and worn out. Slowly Shez stood up, holding on to her son. The doctor sat down, an exhausted figure with the whole world weighing on his shoulders. He managed a weak smile. "We've had a hard time with Awais—but we have managed to save his life."

Shez collapsed back into the chair, tears flowing freely. Salman was crying too as he put an arm around her. "Thank you and all of your people, Doctor," he said.

"He will live," Mubarak went on. "However, the stroke ruptured certain blood vessels to the brain. That is what a stroke is. There was a complete blockage when I first saw him. We have managed to relieve the blockage and restart normal blood flow."

"He will make a full recovery?" Salman asked.

The doctor shook his head. "Only time can tell. Awais will be paralyzed on his right side, and his speech will be a problem, at least for a while. But he has a naturally strong constitution. With the right treatments, physical therapy, and a careful diet, he might come back to 90 percent of normal functioning, perhaps even 100 percent. As of now, we cannot predict how much movement and speech he will regain."

Shez wiped at her eyes. "Can we see him?"

"He is being moved to the step-down unit now. Once he's settled, you may go in for a short visit. He can nod and blink, but he can't speak very much. That will come back to him in stages." Mubarak stood and wiped his brow with a sleeve. "I can tell you this, most patients do not recover from such a massive stroke—and it was massive. But Awais has a great will to live. That's going to make a difference. He's going to be sick for some weeks. However, once he's back home and in familiar surroundings, I think he will defy the odds."

"He always has," Shez whispered.

∝∞∝

GUL NAWAZ AND ASHRAM were in the black Mercedes staff car, prowling along one of the main arteries. While he spoke on his mobile phone, Nawaz flipped to different news stations on the radio.

"With these bombings coming on the heels of the shocking incident at the Sufi shrine," one newsman breathlessly reported, "people on the street tell us they are more fearful than ever. At this hour, the city of Lahore is full of terror and uncertainty." Nothing was known of the attackers except the obvious, that they were a ruthless murder squad. "Of course the Pakistani Taliban are instant suspects, especially with the similarity these bombings have with those at the shrine."

"One initial report from the shopping plaza," a Geo News reporter noted, "claims that the suicide bomber might have been wearing some sort of uniform, perhaps that of a policeman or even a soldier. However, we have no confirmation of that."

There were as yet no preliminary estimates of the dead from the two locations. "Perhaps hundreds have been killed," a studio anchorman ventured, "and many more injured, among them law enforcement, firefighters, and emergency medical workers."

Adding to the Götterdämmerung atmosphere, parts of Lahore began losing electric power as unscheduled load-shedding kicked in.

Nawaz finished his mobile calls and rang off. "Daniyal is on his way to the Student Center, and it is filled with college kids."

"Allah helps his earnest servants," Ashram remarked. He pointed as they passed a police roadblock being set up on a side street. "As if that's going to do them any good!"

"The authorities are easily confused," Nawaz said disdainfully.

He knew what he was talking about. As a terrorist operative, Gul Nawaz had made a friend of chaos and consternation, often confusing the enemy to the point of immobility. With the Lahore operation, starting with the shrine, he was at the top of his malevolent game. The three new targets would produce a carpet of death and destruction that would overwhelm authorities. It was a model of battlefield operations in the art of guerrilla warfare. Gul Nawaz's reward for such service to jihad would not be merely spiritual. He would be adding to his bank account in Tehran.

∞

KAMRAN ARRIVED AT the Student Center and cut through the lobby crowded with young people and faculty. He headed into the busy cafeteria, where he grabbed a booth while one was still available. Many students taking late classes, as well as those headed for adult-education lectures, often ate dinner here in the early evening. It was cheap self-service, and the food wasn't bad. Like most large institutions in Pakistan, the college had its own backup power plant to cover outages, though the lights sometimes ran dim and computer speed dropped to a crawl. There was an impressive glass wall separating the cafeteria from the cavernous lobby, which allowed Kamran to keep a sharp eye out for his party.

While waiting, he made a nervous call on his mobile. "It's me, Sallu. Anything new on Abba?"

"Yes!" the older brother responded excitedly. "He's going to make it, Kam. He's going to make it!."

Kamran took in a long breath and then let it out. "Thank God."

"And thank the doctors! Are you still meeting with Rania and her folks?"

"They should be here any minute. How's mother?"

"She's . . . managing. We're going to see Abba in a little while. You've heard about the explosions?"

"I caught some of it on TV back at the dorm."

There was a long pause before Salman said, "Let us not worry about what we can't control. Concentrate on impressing your future in-laws. I have to go. Ammi needs me. Have a good meeting. Call me when you're free."

Moments later, Kamran spotted Rania and her parents coming in through the lobby doors. He got to his feet and straightened his tie. He had worn his one good suit for the occasion.

The immaculately charming Dr. Omar shook hands warmly. "Hello, Kamran. I'd like to introduce my wife, Lubna."

"Nice to see you, Mrs. Omar. Thanks for coming."

She was in her late forties but looked younger and wore the stylish New York fashions from her own upscale boutique. "I'm so pleased to finally meet you, my dear Kami. Rania has told me so much about you."

"I hope she hasn't oversold me."

Rania chuckled. "No, I only said you were an angel, that's all. Just an angel."

While they got settled in the booth and Rania went off to fetch a pot of tea, Mrs. Omar inquired about Awais. "They said on the news that he was still in critical condition."

"I just found out he's going to pull through."

"That *is* a relief," Dr. Omar said.

"Our prayers are with your father and your family," his wife added.

"All of Lahore is praying for your father."

"It has been a great support to my mother knowing that so many people care."

Rania returned with a large teapot and cups. She poured everyone a serving and sat down modestly but firmly next to Kamran.

"Mr. Reza is out of danger," her mother informed her. "He's going to pull through."

"That's wonderful news, Kami. Thanks be to God."

"I see they've started in with the bombings again," Dr. Omar said.

Mrs. Omar touched her husband's arm. "Jamal, we're not here to talk about such dreadful things. We're here to talk about something joyous and wonderful—marriage." She smiled. "Kamran, you're an intelligent, handsome young man. Everyone who knows you speaks highly of you. My daughter has fallen in love with you. That's enough for us. Jamal and I would be honored to have you as a son-in-law."

Kamran looked at Rania. "I am honored that you think I'm worthy of your family."

"I want you to know," Dr. Omar said, "that all of this terrible stuff about your brother Dani does not reflect on you or your family. Dani is an adult and has made his own choices. From what Rania has told us and what they've been saying on the news, your father is an honorable citizen. It is a great injustice that he was thrown in jail and subjected to such harsh treatment. He might still have to go on trial."

"One of the human rights groups started a web site for his defense fund," Rania said. "Abba made a large contribution."

"That's very kind, sir. Thank you."

"It probably won't go to trial," Dr. Omar said. "The prosecutor sees how public opinion is going. He knows he has no evidence. He'll drop the charges when he can do it gracefully."

"He'll have to," declared his wife. "The state can't afford to be on the losing side of this one." She turned to Kamran. "Do you plan on ultimately practicing law here in Lahore?"

"There'll be two lawyers in the family. Lahore would be our first choice, but we'll probably have to go wherever we can find suitable positions."

"We could end up here or in Islamabad or Karachi," Rania said.

"My real aim is to get into the government in some capacity where I can do the most good for the greatest number of people. Some power position where I can contribute to a better society. Sounds pretentious, I know, but . . . "

"We certainly need a change in this country," Rania's father said. "And it's only going to come from you and your generation. Us old folks, we've had our chance and made a mess of it. We've barely managed to muddle through, as the British say. That's not going to cut it for Pakistan in the twenty-first century."

∽

THE BLACK MERCEDES staff car was parked in the school's main parking lot, less than a soccer field's length from the Student Center. Gul Nawaz was on his mobile while Ashram kept a close watch on the glass-and-brick building.

"We've got a problem," Nawaz said as he put away the phone and turned on the car radio. "They know about the army uniforms."

Within a few minutes, the news was reporting the latest development. "Survivors at the plaza food court," the announcer was saying, "have told investigators that the suicide bomber was dressed as a soldier. It now appears that he arrived at the club on a motor scooter. It was that scooter that blew up and killed, at last count, ten emergency-service workers. It was a double bombing, just as was carried out later at the police station."

Nawaz turned down the radio and looked at the dashboard clock. "Daniyal will be here any minute."

"Amir, today we have already surpassed the feat at the Sufi shrine. If Daniyal's mission is thwarted somehow, it will be no reflection on your command."

"There is no reason it should be thwarted," Nawaz insisted. "As we figured in the planning sessions, the army is seen on campus since the crackdown started. He won't draw attention just being in uniform. He'll accomplish the mission. Daniyal is the most dedicated of our martyrs."

Ashram nodded past the windshield. "There he is now."

Nawaz's lazy eye was active and all-seeing as he peered at the figure on the motor scooter approaching the rear of the Student Center. "Our work here is done. Hassan will handle the second bomb. Let's get to the airfield. The plane is waiting."

As he had been instructed, Daniyal Reza parked the motor scooter near the bike rack behind the Student Center. As he dismounted, his movements were awkward, and he had to stand by the scooter for a moment to steady himself. The explosive packs under the uniform had become heavier as the minutes had worn on. He lifted the seat and took out the textbook that completed his charade. His hands were shaking slightly, but he was in firm control of himself.

"I pray," he whispered, "for the strength to carry out this last act in Allah's honor."

With a stern bearing, Daniyal stepped around the corner of the building. He could feel the electrical wires inside his pocket loosening from the tape that held them to the microswitch. He stopped and adjusted the wire and tape. Finally Daniyal assumed the squared-off posture of a proud soldier.

Only a few moments more, and he would be in the presence of God. "The glory, the glory, the *glory*," he chanted under his breath.

Two private security guards were standing by the entrance to the lobby. Daniyal blended in with a noisy group of students going through the revolving doors. When several of them laughed over something, Daniyal joined in and made it look like he was part of the group. The security guards ignored him. He moved quickly among the people who were sitting and standing around, talking animatedly. There were long lines at the information booth and the dean's desk. Through the glass wall, Daniyal could see the crowded cafeteria.

He took up a central position and put his hand into a pocket, then threw the textbook aside. *"God is great!"* he bellowed.

He pressed the microswitch.

Nothing happened.

Then came the screaming and people jamming the exit.

Panicking, Daniyal ripped open his pocket and grabbed at a loose wire.

One of the security guards came running. He launched himself at the soldier and tackled him. The two went tumbling across the floor. The guard was trying to pin Daniyal's hands. With a burst of ferocious strength, Daniyal heaved the man away and got to his feet.

He fumbled in his pocket.

The sharp blast was fiery and full of steel pieces. Instantly, along with others, Daniyal Reza was no more. He had served his purpose on earth.

Cruising in the black Mercedes staff car some blocks away, Gul Nawaz and his driver heard the explosion. The amir pressed his palms together. "I pray that Allah will accept Dani Reza as one of his most worthy servants."

"It will surely be so," the driver said.

TWENTY

Peace is its own reward.

MAHATMA GANDHI

Twenty-four hours later, Kamran Reza regained consciousness to find himself a patient in a private room at University Hospital. He could hazily see his brother Salman across the room, talking with a nurse. When Kamran groaned out a few words, they both came to his bedside.

Salman pulled a chair over. "You have a minor concussion, but the doctor says nothing permanent."

Kamran sat up, rubbing his eyes. He spotted a decanter of water on the side table and poured a glass. He downed a big swallow. "That helps."

"The doctor said you can go home tomorrow. Feel like talking?"

Kamran held his head. "Tell me slowly. What about Rania and her parents?"

"They're okay. Her father had some glass removed from his arm. Rania and her mother made it through with just a few bruises. The cafeteria's glass wall was blown out. They say nine were killed there, and twenty-three in the lobby. A lot of injuries too."

"I can remember hearing the explosion and then nothing. How is Abba doing?"

"He doesn't look all that wonderful at the moment. But the doctor says he'll get better day by day. The main thing is that we have him back."

Kamran said, "That's twice he's come back from the dead."

"That's right. First Bangladesh, and now this."

Kamran sank into the pillow. He felt his head.

"You haven't seen the latest news," Salman said. "They're treating Awais Reza like some kind of hero who has been unjustly treated."

"I guess they see Abba as another victim of this country of ours. How is Ammi taking it?"

"She cries sometimes, but that will stop as soon as Abba gets home from the hospital next week. Of course she's grieving for Dani. They released a video confession he made. They say he was the one who blew himself up at your school. How's that for brutal irony? Our brother a suicide bomber. As hard as that is to—" Salman choked up. "As hard as that is to accept."

Kamran reached out and took his brother's hand.

After a long moment of silence, the older brother said, "I've got some good news for you. I got a call from Zain this morning. You met Zalman Khan, the lawyer representing Abba?"

"Yes."

"Well, according to Zain, he heard from one of the professors that Khan's firm is going to offer you a trainee position."

Kamran slowly lifted himself up.

"Zain says the professor will arrange an interview for you as soon as you're up to it."

"Salman, I'd never have gotten to this point without the support of you and our folks. But what about you? With Abba laid up and Ammi caring for him, you'll have no one to help at the shop. It'll all be on you."

Salman waved off the thought. "A lot of shop owners work all day. Abba did for years. I can handle it for as long as it takes him to recover. He'll be back at work in no time. You'll see."

"Perhaps you're right. The Anarkali bazaar has been too much of his life for too long. He will never give it up. Besides, he's too young to retire."

Salman reached over and put a hand on his brother's shoulder. "We'll get through this horrible time. Besides, what the hell is the alternative?"

TWENTY-ONE

Every day has been so short, every hour so fleeting,
every minute so filled with the life I love
that time for me has fled on too swift a wing.

AGA KHAN III

In the weeks that followed the mass bombings in Lahore, the Pakistani government, and ISI in particular, were vilified for their inability to hunt down the leaders of the Taliban front that had carried out the attacks—especially the notorious Gul Nawaz, who had been operating freely in Pakistan and Afghanistan for years. Nawaz had executed his mission in Lahore and promptly vanished. Washington once again began pushing Islamabad to root out its clandestine links to insurgent groups, and government officials once again were adamant in their insistence that no such links existed. In other words, it was business as usual.

"I have lost interest in what our current government is or isn't doing," Awais told Salman. He was in the living room, comfortably ensconced in his new leather recliner, offered in exchange for an interview with a local TV station. "Judging from the papers and all this stuff on TV, it seems that everyone has finally given up completely on our so-called leaders. We must have hope for the next election, Sallu. This is always the hope of Pakistan's people: a leader who will lead with a clear conscience."

Salman strode around the living room. "Come, Abba. We have had too much sadness. Let us put on a happy face."

"This *is* my happy face."

"We have a lot to be grateful for, Abba. For one thing, they have dropped those ridiculous charges they cooked up."

"Yes, for that I am certainly grateful."

"But look at us now. You have gained much popularity. We suddenly have more customers than ever before. People come to the Anarkali bazaar to seek out Awais Reza's shop. Like it is a brand name."

"Yes, it's a real break for us in this economy."

Salman clapped. "And the best luck of all, Abba! Kamran is marrying a fine lady from a wonderful family. It is a blessing! And let us speak plainly. As we very well know, Kami is marrying upward in class. That means we are all stepping up in the world."

"I am pleased for you and your brother. But your mother and I are content to just be ourselves. Who knows, maybe someday the sky will fall and you too will find a wife."

Salman shrugged. "In time, no doubt. But right now, I like my freedom too much."

"I still think you ought to consider our old friend Noor's pretty niece, the one with the 'camel eyes,' as you call them. She's been sweet on you for years."

"Yes, she's a definite . . . maybe. But let us marry off one son at a time."

Awais cocked an ear to the shouts of children playing in the alley. "I don't think it's too early to hope for future grandchildren, yes?"

"Rania and Kami are career-oriented, Abba, but they also want to start a family. I predict the first baby will be along sooner rather than later. Rania has said as much."

"That was a wonderful time, Salman. When you boys were little. I remember how you were always playing with the TV controls, looking for your cartoon shows. You had to find cartoons or you'd start bawling your head off. And Kami was always begging for candy!"

Salman broke up laughing. "A while back I gave him a batch of Hasan's smuggled Hershey bars, and his eyes lit up like he was six years old."

"That's Kamran, all right. I remember how you and Dani—" Awais broke off but kept his composure. It was how he coped, steeling his emotions, keeping control. He had already cried the tears of a bereaved parent, the tears of a devastated father who felt he had somehow failed to provide the guidance and wisdom that might have kept his son from the clutches of those bent on using violence to achieve . . . to achieve what? For the old lance corporal, the wanton killing of innocent civilians could never be justified. He had seen such horrors in Bangladesh, and it had soured his soul then as it did now. The fact that his own flesh and blood had been part of the terror madness was a sin the Reza family could never erase.

"Come on, Abba. Let's not dwell on the past. Think of your grandkids."

"I must take some responsibility for Daniyal," Awais went on, almost to himself. "I failed him."

"That's not so."

"I'm afraid it is. If I had not been so wrapped up in making a success of my father's shop, I would have done a better job raising him. My father did well by me, and I thought I was doing the right thing by my own sons. You and Kamran have become fine young men, but Dani became . . . a *monster*. I don't really understand that."

"You and mother did not fail Dani! He failed you."

Awais shook his head sadly. "I should have seen how extreme he had become. Actually, I did see it. Why didn't I *do* something!"

"Abba, no one could have foreseen what they were up to at that madrassa." Salman sat down next to Awais. "Daniyal made his own choices. May I recall for you the holy Quran and the Prophet Noah? When Noah felt guilty and was repenting because his son had gone astray, God reminded Noah that each of us is responsible for our actions. As it was with Noah's son, so it was with Daniyal."

"I know this in my head, Salman. But not in my heart."

Salman went back to pacing. "Have you taken your pills?"

"Oh, yes. Your mother keeps me on schedule." He chuckled. "She's a very stern nurse, I'll have you know." Awais flexed an arm. "My strength is coming back very quickly now. You saw how I hauled in those heavy boxes at the shop yesterday. I'll be back to my old schedule pretty soon."

"No need to rush it, Abba. I can handle the shop until you're feeling up to regular hours."

Awais smiled. "You're a good son, Salman. I know the business will be in capable hands for many years to come."

"Years we will share together, Abba." Salman winked. "According to the doctor, you're not exactly over the hill just yet."

☙❧

SHEZ REZA HAD BEEN warmly invited back to work at the hospital. The head nurse stopped by the house to apologize in person for the unwarranted suspension they had imposed. "It was a stupid mistake, and I told the admin people that at the time." Shez was touched by the visit and assured the head nurse that she would be glad to return to work, but that for a while she would be taking care of Awais full time at home. As the head nurse was leaving, she took notice of Awais's prescribed medication. The next day, a delivery came from the hospital; it was a six-month supply of Awais's medicine. Shez sent a large bouquet of pink carnations to the nurses' station.

She had always known Awais was strong in body and mind, but in the weeks after his release from the hospital, he had shown a truly remarkable stamina and power of recovery. After only ten days of bed rest, he was up and around almost as normal. He was walking well, and his speech was perfect. "Your blood pressure is almost normal. Heart rate also normal. You've lost a few kilos you didn't need anyway. It's a miracle, my darling husband, but you're in better shape now than you were after walking all across India."

"And I feel a lot better now than I did after that little hike."

Awais and Shez had told their two sons that their shame over Daniyal was not going to define the rest of their lives. "We must walk always in the path of righteousness," Shez had said. "What we do in life will show to all who we are."

In private, the parents shared their grief and blamed themselves for their son's wayward path to destruction. They vowed to say a prayer of repentance every day for the lives Daniyal had taken, including his own.

In her private prayers offered to the East, Shez gave thanks for the family's newfound hope for the future. She always ended her prayers, often in tears, by asking for God's forgiveness for the innocent lives lost in her son's warped attempt to serve his faith.

∽

IN THE WEEKS leading up to Kamran and Rania's wedding, public life in and around Lahore was beginning to pick up again. With the military and police checkpoints finally disappearing from around the city, people were again out and about, going to the malls, filling up the restaurants, strolling the spacious parks. The newspapers and TV reports still carried pictures of Gul Nawaz and his Talibani circle. The story was the same as it always seemed to be: no high-ranking terrorists involved in the recent bombings had been brought to ground. The picture painted by the media was very clear—the major terror groups were not being disrupted at all but were still actively operating, recruiting, and growing in strength. The old charge that elements of the government were secretly supporting certain extremist fronts was by now routinely reported and as routinely denied.

"The upshot of all this murkiness and ineptitude," a Geo News reporter told his audience, "is that Nawaz and his ilk have once again killed innocent people inside our country, including a number of teenagers, and have gotten away scot-free."

Be that as it may, the Anarkali bazaar was once more the scene of crowded shopping lanes, customers lingering around the stalls and cart vendors or pausing for a neighborly chat and an iced drink. It was a marketplace life that had existed for hundreds of years. The bazaar was one of Lahore's great communal traditions, part of the city's unofficial infrastructure. Shoppers might stay away in times of increased tension and fear, but they seldom stayed away for long.

It was what Pakistanis seemed to do best, coming back from the brink time and time again. Through tragedy and catastrophe, wars and floods, assassinations and police crackdowns, weak and corrupt leadership, the people of Pakistan knew only that they must keep marching on toward a better future. They were all driven by one idea—what Pakistan could become someday.

After leaving the hospital, Kamran spent a couple of nights at his parents' house. As part of the healing process, they joined together in prayers of sorrow and devotion as well as of gratitude for the goodwill that had come their way. They did not avoid speaking of the departed one, but neither did they dwell on his savage act of self-destruction.

Kamran and Rania met for an hour at their secret spot in the park. Hidden under the sheltering boughs, they embraced sweetly, though it was against Muslim custom and marital tradition. "We were spared when others were not," Kamran said. "For that, I am self-centered enough to be very grateful."

They sat down in the grass close to each other.

"When my mother and I saw you in the hospital, you were pretty down. She says you're feeling guilty because of what Daniyal did."

He looked up through the trees and shook his head. "My own brother!"

"You were brothers, yes, but you did not share the same spirit and soul. You and Dani are total opposites. He may have been brainwashed, but he acted of his own accord."

"I had a bad feeling about him the last couple of years. I told you six months ago that I was afraid he'd fall in with the extremists. Remember? Those so-called religious retreats? You can bet those were terrorist training missions."

They sat in silence except for the muted din of city traffic and the chirping of the birds. Kamran took Rania's hand and squeezed it.

"God has tested our love," she said quietly, "and given His approval. We will grow together. Let us never lose sight of that."

"Never."

Rania perked up. "So, my dear one, are you getting nervous?"

"About us taking the nikkah vows? Yes, I'm a little nervous. Why? Are you getting nervous?"

"No, I've felt good about everything ever since my parents woke up and realized what a good choice I made for a husband. I study as much as I can, but I'm too excited to concentrate. Besides, my mother has me doing a lot of errands for the wedding. I'm into my fourth fitting for my gown and dealing with all of the bridesmaids. Talk about finicky women! Your mother told me you're wearing a traditional off-white sharvani. I approve. It's a stately look, especially on certain handsome young men."

"If you say so. To me it's all a little too, well, ethnic. I mean with the medieval trench-coat thing, like Vlad the Impaler. And the cute little matching hat."

"It's called a kula."

"And those Punjabi sandals I have to wear! Way too feminine for a masculine fellow like me, no?"

Rania laughed. "Those are called chappals, and they're adorable, even on a macho guy like you. And think of the future. You want to get into politics eventually. When the time comes, it won't hurt to have a wedding photo that shows you as a true son of Pakistan. It's the same formal dress Pakistan's founder always wore."

"You know," he said, "you'd make a darn good campaign manager."

"I'm going to be pretty busy just being a wife." Rania had to rush off to one of her mother's jewelry vendors to pick out some items for her wedding ensemble. "Everything on loan, of course. I'm going to look a lot richer than we really are."

"Believe me, so am I."

Back at his desk in his dorm room, Kamran was greeted affectionately by Zain. "It's good to have you back at home base. There's a basket of get-well cards waiting for you down at the mail desk."

"I can't tell you how much all the support has meant to our family. People died because of what my brother did, yet they haven't turned against us."

"That is because of your father, Kam. He has become known as a courageous citizen."

"Yes, and we're all proud of him."

"He stands by his principles, a model for the nation. What Daniyal and the others did does not change that."

Kamran took a deep breath. "I never really thought he'd go all the way with this jihad business. I saw it coming, but I didn't believe it would actually happen." He shook his head. "With me and Rania's family sitting a hundred feet away!"

Zain took the chair next to the desk. "I probably shouldn't bring this up, but we have a history of indulging each other in our vain attempts to understand what it's all about. Right?"

"Right."

"It's a very simple proposition—by your brother killing innocent people, has God turned a cold eye on the Reza family? I ask only as an intellectual point, you see."

Kamran took the point and focused on it with narrowing eyes. "I don't see that he has turned a cold eye on our family. Things are better for all of us now."

"So maybe God approves of Daniyal's martyrdom."

Kamran threw up his hands. "I'm not a mystic or a cleric, only a humble law student. I have no brief to offer the court, your honor. Actually, my mother has always said that God was watching over the Rezas, and Rania says God is watching over us. I know Him only as a fair God, ready to offer mercy and forgiveness. I accept His judgment on our family, whatever it may be."

ஜ

THE LATE-SUMMER WEDDING of Kamran Reza and Rania Omar was a family and social event as well as a wedding. Work crews were brought in to pitch eight large field tents in and around the

Omars' spacious gardens, each open-air rigging done up in an ar-
ray of "happy colors." Some tents were for meeting and socializing,
others for dining and dancing. The central structure, where the formal ceremony would be performed, was a huge Arabic marquee,
nearly the size of a circus tent, with a canopied entrance and silk
flying banners. Inside, there was seating for well over two hundred.
The elevated dais was encircled by rows of red tulips and set off by a
background of flashing silk colors.

By 10:00 on the morning of the wedding, over a hundred men,
women, and children were already swarming over the grounds, with
more guests arriving every few minutes. From one of the shady tents,
a tabla and sitar group played traditional tunes, the evocative melo-
dies mixing well with the warm breeze and drifting incense. Grilled
snacks and cold drinks were being dispensed to appease those who
couldn't wait till later for the main meal. A refrigerated truck stood
off to the side, loaded with bottles of Pepsi and 7Up. A staff of valets
was out front in the circular driveway to greet guests and attend to
parking. Up at the house, the catering staff had taken over the large
kitchen before dawn to assemble the elaborate wedding feast. The
head chef hovered over his cooks and fussed over the details. There
were chicken, lamb, and beef kabob dishes to finish as well as the fin-
est biryani rice, cauliflower, potato and spinach concoctions, sweet
treats, and candied fruits.

When the Reza family arrived, they were all ushered straight
into the house, where a private suite had been set aside for their use.
The groom looked very formal and serious in his below-the-knee
sharvani coat in off-white satin, elaborately embroidered in black
with arabesque swirls. "This is the most dressed-up I've ever had to
be," Kamran complained. "Or ever want to be." Awais and Salman
wore similar long coats but with less embroidery. The proud father,

eight weeks after his stroke, beamed with healthy coloring and a joyous spirit.

Before noon, some two hundred chattering guests, relatives, and extended-family members, as well as the officiating cleric, had assembled in the marquee tent and were gleefully awaiting the bride and groom. But first the nikkah contract would be signed, a legal matter similar to a Western-style prenuptial agreement but dealing mostly with inheritance laws. In addition to the couple's signatures, four witnesses were required in order for the nikkah contract to be valid: two from the bride's family and two from the groom's. As was the usual practice, the two sets of parents stood as witnesses for their children.

When the four parents finally entered the crowded tent and took seats on the platform, it was amid polite clapping and murmurs of approval, everything captured by two still photographers and two videographers. Mrs. Omar blew kisses, and her husband waved. Someone called out Awais's name and he stood to take a bow as the assembled guests gave him a hearty round of applause.

After the ceremony of marriage, the formal signing of the contract, the feasting with friends, and the bubble of festivities, Kamran slipped away to change into the more comfortable clothes he'd brought along for the dinner and reception. The house was quiet as he hurried to a private room and changed from the heavy satin coat to a white cotton shirt and slacks. He threw off the "magic-carpet driver" shoes and donned his comfortable loafers. On his way back through the house, he was stopped by Rania's father in the hallway. "My son!" he sang out, wrapping an arm around Kamran's shoulder. "Come, let us have a private word. They stepped into a side room. "You have made my daughter happy, and that means everything to her mother and me. You know Rania's a headstrong girl. We've always worried she'd never find a husband to match her sheer brain-power, to say nothing of her willpower."

"I hope you know, sir, that Rania's happiness means everything to me also. As for the brainpower, frankly, I've got all I can do to keep up with her."

Dr. Omar grinned. "I know what you mean, but from now on, that's your job, not mine." He reached inside the jacket of his London-made suit and took out something hidden in his palm. "Now, look, son, I decided not to go into this with your father, but I have made a decision. As you know, it is customary for the groom's family to pro-vide a dowry of some sort. Awais has told us he has gathered some jewelry and cash for this purpose."

"Yes, that's so."

"Kamran, I wish him to hold on to those valuables. Instead, al-low me to provide the dowry, the money you and Rania will have to start your marriage on the right foot. Here, this is for you." Omar handed Kamran a check. "This is money I have long saved for just this day."

With that, the two men embraced, happy and tired at the end of a day that had blended tradition and modernity, Islamic ritual and London-cut suits, ebullient good wishes for the future and the unspoken sadness of the recent past hidden only barely behind the day's bright colors and sounds. The Omars and Rezas had given their blessing to a new family—that of Kamran and Rania—and had invested in it their hope for a fine future. It was a time-honored blessing, made all the more profound by the shared knowledge that families, like entire nations, must sometimes have to withstand the toughest trials and endure almost beyond endurance.

Acknowledgments

I am deeply grateful to many individuals for their support of this project. To begin with, I am forever indebted to the Reza family and the residents of Anarkali and greater Lahore.

In particular, my heartfelt thanks go to Mumtaz Ahmad, Wajahat Ali, Mohsin Hamid, Mosharraf Zaidi, Faran Tahir, Haroon Moghul, Peter Bergen, Rashid Hussein, Akbar Ahmad, Vali Nasr, Cameron Munter, Marilyn Wyatt, Parag Khanna, Mirza Baig, Mona Malik, Reza Aslan, Haris Tarin, Sarah Kureshi, Eboo Patel, Jeremy Rosner, and Uzma Sabir. The views expressed in this book do not represent the U.S. State Department or its policies.

Thanks to Steve Petruso for his sustained counsel and for his aid in completing this project.

I am indebted to Clive Priddle at PublicAffairs for his wonderful commitment, ideas, and patience with shaping the work and always providing excellent feedback. The entire team at PublicAffairs, including Emily Lavelle, Michelle Welsh-Horst, Lindsay Fradkoff, Maria Goldverg, and Peggy Garry has shown great care and expertise throughout the process.

Thanks to Don Fehr, my agent at Trident Media Group, for his continued belief in the importance of the project.

Lastly, during the long period it took me to research and write this book, my family has been wonderfully supportive. As the great poet Muhammad Iqbal (1877–1938) wrote, "You are an eagle, and your station is much higher than the royal palaces—beyond the mountains and higher." I am grateful to my wife, Ambereen, for her unwavering faith in and care for my academic endeavors as well as for her generosity and forbearance. I thank my loving parents, Dr. Kaleem and Zarfshan Ullah, for inspiring us with an appreciation of poetry and Allama Iqbal—and for setting a high bar for civic activism and scholarship while providing the best role models one could ask for. To my in-laws, Dr. Sheba Khalid and M. Khalid Shaffie, I owe thanks for their good humor and invaluable support. To my energetic siblings, Sarah, Noor, Imran, and Muneer, for their constant help on the project. Special thanks to my lovely sister Sarah for her inspiration and to my patient brother Noor for his encouragement throughout the long process. To all, I extend my deepest gratitude.

Haroon K. Ullah is a Pakistani American scholar, diplomat, and field researcher specializing in South Asia and the Middle East. He grew up in a farming community in Washington state and was trained at Harvard University's John F. Kennedy School of Government, where he served as a senior fellow and completed his MPA. He was a William J. Fulbright Fellow, a Harvard University Presidential Scholar, and a National Security Education Program Fellow.

PublicAffairs is a publishing house founded in 1997. It is a tribute to the standards, values, and flair of three persons who have served as mentors to countless reporters, writers, editors, and book people of all kinds, including me.

I. F. STONE, proprietor of *I. F. Stone's Weekly*, combined a commitment to the First Amendment with entrepreneurial zeal and reporting skill and became one of the great independent journalists in American history. At the age of eighty, Izzy published *The Trial of Socrates*, which was a national bestseller. He wrote the book after he taught himself ancient Greek.

BENJAMIN C. BRADLEE was for nearly thirty years the charismatic editorial leader of *The Washington Post*. It was Ben who gave the *Post* the range and courage to pursue such historic issues as Watergate. He supported his reporters with a tenacity that made them fearless and it is no accident that so many became authors of influential, best-selling books.

ROBERT L. BERNSTEIN, the chief executive of Random House for more than a quarter century, guided one of the nation's premier publishing houses. Bob was personally responsible for many books of political dissent and argument that challenged tyranny around the globe. He is also the founder and longtime chair of Human Rights Watch, one of the most respected human rights organizations in the world.

•   •   •

For fifty years, the banner of Public Affairs Press was carried by its owner Morris B. Schnapper, who published Gandhi, Nasser, Toynbee, Truman, and about 1,500 other authors. In 1983, Schnapper was described by *The Washington Post* as "a redoubtable gadfly." His legacy will endure in the books to come.

Peter Osnos, *Founder and Editor-at-Large*